CAMBRIDGE SKILLS FOR FLUENCY
Series editor: Adrian Doff

Reading 4

Simon Greenall
Diana Pye

CAMBRIDGE
UNIVERSITY PRESS

Published by the Press Syndicate of the University of Cambridge
The Pitt Building, Trumpington Street, Cambridge CB2 1RP
40 West 20th Street, New York, NY 10011–4211, USA
10 Stamford Road, Oakleigh, Melbourne 3166, Australia

© Cambridge University Press 1993

First published 1993

Printed in Great Britain
by Scotprint Ltd, Musselburgh, Scotland

ISBN 0 521 43869 1

Contents

Map of the book

Unit	Functions/Structural areas	Vocabulary areas	Reading strategies
1 Odd socks		Clothes, feelings.	Predicting; reading for specific information; evaluating the text; dealing with unfamiliar words; text organisation; understanding the writer's style; reacting to the text.
2 Lessons in German	Describing a sequence of events.	School trip.	Predicting; reading for specific information; evaluating the text; dealing with unfamiliar words; understanding the writer's style.
3 I can't get rid of the smell of burning	Talking about past events; describing feelings and impressions; past tenses.	Fire.	Reading for specific information; evaluating the text; dealing with unfamiliar words; understanding text organisation; inferring.
4 Imperial English	Talking about the past and present; past simple, present perfect, present simple and continuous.	Science.	Extracting main ideas; dealing with unfamiliar words; inferring; reacting to the text.
5 Just another Saturday as a sheep in wolves' clothing	Describing behaviour; present tenses.	Football.	Predicting; reading for specific information; dealing with unfamiliar words; reacting to the text; inferring; understanding the writer's style.
6 We've never had it so bad	Talking about feelings; discussing values; passive voice.	Teenagers.	Predicting; extracting main ideas; evaluating the text.
7 In affection and esteem	Speculating; making arrangements.		Predicting; reading for specific information; inferring; reacting to the text.
8 Help! I'm turning into my dad	Telling a story; describing behaviour.	Family holidays.	Predicting; extracting main ideas; dealing with unfamiliar words; evaluating the text.
9 True stories		News items.	Reacting to the text; extracting main ideas; inferring; reacting to the text.

Unit	Functions/Structural areas	Vocabulary areas	Reading strategies
10 Friendship	Talking about the past; describing feelings; past tenses.	Personal relationships.	Reading for specific information; extracting main information; dealing with unfamiliar words.
11 New face of ageism	Describing appearance and stereotypes.	Old age.	Predicting; extracting main ideas; dealing with unfamiliar words; reading for specific information.
12 My favourite place	Describing places; describing atmosphere and impressions.	City scenes.	Predicting; understanding the writer's style; dealing with unfamiliar words; reading for specific information; inferring.
13 Home town	Describing people and places.	People and places.	Evaluating the text; dealing with unfamiliar words; inferring; reading for specific information; reacting to the text; understanding the writer's style.
14 Looking for a rain god	Describing places; describing human reactions.	African bush drought.	Predicting; dealing with unfamiliar words; reading for specific information; evaluating the text.
15 Mirror	Describing appearance; talking about the passage of time.	Facial features.	Reading for specific information; extracting main ideas; dealing with unfamiliar words; reacting to the text.
16 Colours	Describing national preferences.	Colour taste and fashion.	Reading for specific information; dealing with unfamiliar words; text organisation.
17 The new world	Telling a story; present tenses.		Predicting; reading for specific information; reacting to the text.
18 Take my tip	Describing customs; stating opinions.	Tipping habits.	Extracting main ideas; reading for specific information; dealing with unfamiliar words.
19 Pilgrim at Tinker Creek	Describing sights and sounds; describing atmosphere and impressions.	Wildlife and the river bank.	Text organisation; predicting; inferring; understanding the writer's style.
20 The new café	Describing people and places; telling a story; describing feelings.	Personal relationships.	Extracting main ideas; understanding the writer's style.

Thanks

We would like to thank:

Jeanne McCarten, Alison Silver, Lindsay White, Peter Ducker, Amanda Ogden and everybody at Cambridge University Press for making this book possible.

Adrian Doff and the other readers for their extremely helpful comments on the first draft.

The authors and publishers would like to thank the following teachers and their students for piloting *Reading 4*:

Mick Davies, EF International School, Cambridge; Michael Jenkins, The British School, Milan; Ruth Jimack, The British Council, Athens; Teresa Lopez, Barcelona; Elspeth Mackay, IH Language School, Budapest; David Moreton, Bell College, Saffron Walden; Lynda Newbery, Filton Technical College, Bristol; Tony Robinson, Eurocentre, Cambridge.

Their detailed comments and constructive suggestions made an invaluable contribution to this book.

1 | Odd socks

1 What sort of things annoy you or go wrong in your everyday life? Think about, for example, coat hangers, sticky tape, pieces of string, photocopiers or automatic vending machines. Make a list and say why they annoy you.

2 Look at the titles of the unit, article and poem:

Odd socks   The odd couple   The Solo Sock

What do you think annoys the writers? Is the subject likely to be treated seriously or humorously?

3 In this article, which appeared in *The Observer*, the writer Richard Brooks uses the term MSS to talk about what annoys him, and suggests a solution and an explanation. Read it and find out what MSS is, and what the solution is.

The odd couple

Richard Brooks on the high divorce rate among socks

I FIRST noticed it about seven or eight years ago. Since then it has got progressively worse and more mysterious. Missing Sock Syndrome is one of *the* afflictions of modern times.

I have my theories about MSS, but, sadly, no real cure. The root of the problem must lie in having a large family. I haven't done a foot count, but there must be more than 100 pairs of socks in my household. Every week, at least one goes missing. Occasionally, days or even weeks later, it turns up.

Sometimes it is discovered stuck in the washing machine, or, more cosily, in the tumble drier. Sometimes it is sighted down the back of a radiator.

But the mystery remains. Why do socks desert their partners, often never to return? And where do they go when they are never found again?

MSS can be alleviated. One colleague says that his decision to remain single has been largely influenced by not wanting to catch MSS. Another has only pairs of blue and red socks; 12 pairs of each colour.

About a year ago, getting increasingly fed up with the syndrome, I went out and bought five pairs of grey socks. Very drab, said my wife. It has helped, though not entirely. Identical pairs, I've discovered, manage to end up with one sock significantly bigger than the other after several washes.

Last week, I asked my youngest daughter, aged six, about missing socks. She had some answers. She looked into her sock drawer, and found three lone socks. To my amazement, she knew the whereabouts of their 'partner'. One was 'in the cellar', another 'at Maxine's' (her best friend), while the third was 'at Aunty Mary's'.

I was stunned at her sock insouciance. Only my nine-year-old daughter shows some early signs of inheriting her father's MSS concerns. My wife thinks I'm a sock bore. But then, I have noticed that my socks regularly turn up on my wife's feet – she is cavalier when it comes to hosiery.

4 Which of the following words would you use to describe the tone of the passage? Can you explain why? You may want to choose more than one word.

> pessimistic   optimistic   humorous   serious   dramatic
> mock-serious   threatening   poetic   ironic   light-hearted

5 The writer uses slightly complex language that suggests that MSS is very serious. Look at these sentences from the article and write them in a simpler way. You may want to use a dictionary to appreciate the nuances of certain words.

1 I haven't done a foot count ...
2 Why do socks desert their partners ... ?
3 MSS can be alleviated.
4 I was stunned at her sock insouciance.
5 ... she is cavalier when it comes to hosiery.

6 Do you think his family shares his concern about MSS? Can you explain why or why not?

7 The poem *The Solo Sock* is by Garrison Keillor, the contemporary American writer and broadcaster. Read the first two stanzas and decide where each line ends. Mark the line endings like this |.

The Solo Sock

Of life's many troubles, I've known quite a few; bad plumbing and earaches and troubles with you, but the saddest of all, when it's all said and done, is to look for your socks and find only one. Here's a series of single socks stacked in a row. Where in the world did their fellow socks go?

About missing socks, we have very few facts. Some say cats steal them to use for backpacks, or desperate Norwegians willing to risk prison to steal socks to make lutefisk. But the robbery theories just don't hold water: why would they take one and not take the odder?

8 **Read the rest of the poem and find out Keillor's solution for what Brooks calls MSS.**

Now, *some* people lose socks, and though you may scoff,
Some go to shows and have their socks knocked off.
Some use a sock to mop up spilled gin with
And some people had just one sock to begin with.
But for most missing socks, or sock migration,
Sockologists have no quick explanation.

Socks *are* independent, studies have shown,
And most feel a need for some time alone.
Some socks are bitter from contact with feet;
Some, seeking holiness, go on retreat;
Some need adventure and cannot stay put;
Some socks feel useless and just underfoot.
But whatever the reason these socks lose control,
Each sock has feelings down deep in its sole.
If you wake in the night and hear creaking and scraping,
It's the sound of a sock, bent on escaping.
The socks on the floor that you think the kids dropped?
They're socks that went halfway, got tired and stopped.

It might help if, every day,
As you don your socks, you take time to say:
"Thank you, dear socks, for a job that is thankless.
You comfort my feet from tiptoe to ankless,
Working in concert a cotton duet,
Keeping them snug and absorbing the sweat,
And yet you smell springlike, a regular balm,
As in Stravinsky's *Le Sacré du Printemps*,
And so I bless you with all my heart
And pray that the two of you never shall part.
I love you, dear socks, you are socko to me,
The most perfect pair that I ever did see.
I thank you and bless you now. *Vobiscum Pax.*"
Then you bend down and put on your socks.

This *may* help, but you must accept
That half of all socks are too proud to be kept,
And, as with children, their leaving is ritual.
Half of all socks need to be individual.

Garrison Keillor

Does the writer think he has totally solved the problem?

9 There are a number of lines in the poem which look as if they rhyme rather strangely. For example, he writes:

> But the robbery theories just don't hold water:
> Why would they take one and not take the odder?

In fact, the word *odder* suggests how some Americans would pronounce that word *other* and make it rhyme with *water*, and also refers to the *odd* sock. Can you find other examples of lines which rhyme because of the way they are pronounced by an American speaker?
    There is one pair of lines which only rhyme because he invents a word. Can you find which it is?
    The writer has also invented some words just for fun. Can you find any?

10 Think about how you would read this poem aloud. Choose from the following adverbs and adverb phrases to describe how you might read each line aloud.

seriously   passionately   slowly   fast   grimly
with a smile   loudly   softly   tensely   in a relaxed way
breathily   in a sing-song way

If you can, try reading the poem aloud in the manner the adverbs suggest.

11 The writers suggest that odd socks have a life of their own. Think about what an odd sock would say if it could talk. Write an interview with the sock in which it explains why it left, where it's been and what it did.

2 | Lessons in German

1 The passage in this unit is about a school exchange in which British schoolchildren visit Germany. What do you expect to happen on such an exchange? What problems might there be?

Did you go on a language exchange when you were at school? If so, what country did you go to? How long did you stay? Who did you stay with? Was it a positive experience? Would you advise young people to do the same?

Tuesday: The first lesson starts at 8am. Is it really such a good idea to start school this early? On the other hand, German children finish at 1pm at the latest. I round up my 20 boys and we set off on our obligatory tour of the Rathaus in Mainz, followed by a visit to the Gutenbergmuseum. Why is the guide's English so good?

By the evening, I think, so far so good. One day gone and no major problems. At 11.15pm a phone call from England. Robert's exchange is not working out. Sleepless night.

Wednesday: Into school for lessons. Chat to Robert. His partner seems to have different interests. Nothing like the lad-about-town impression he gave on his form. Robert is hardly allowed to go out/watch television/eat. Help!

The boys go into lessons with their opposite numbers. I notice, with some envy, that each classroom has an overhead projector, that some teachers arrive at 9.30 and others go home at midday. What am I doing teaching in England? Have animated conversation in the staff room. We get on to the Gulf war. Everyone surprised by what they perceive as British fervour for the war and antipathy for the cautious German approach.

Later in the day I spend 40 minutes on the phone to Robert's German family. They have firm views on family discipline. I find myself negotiating compromise peace terms. A test of my German and diplomatic skills.

Thursday: Learn that the German organiser spent 50 minutes on the phone last

night to aforementioned family. Outing today down the Rhine Valley. Castles to the left and right of us. Magnificent scenery. Our boys are more interested in the girls on the coach. Stop at Bacharach and climb up to the castle on the hill to satisfy German enthusiasm for exercise and fresh air, much to the dismay of 16-year-old English boys.

Stop for lunch in Koblenz. No sign of Tom and David back at the coach. Shouts of "I saw them going into a pub, sir." Twenty minutes later they turn up. "Sorry sir, we turned *rechts* instead of *links*."

Friday: Another day in school. Embark on a positive discussion about the differences between the two countries. German cleanliness, awareness of environmental problems and facilities for

2 Read the passage and find out who the following people are.

- the writer
- Robert
- Tom and David
- Doris and Jürgen

3 The writer goes through a range of emotions during the visit. Write an adjective or two to describe how he is feeling each day.

4 The passage takes the form of a diary kept from day to day. Read it again and look for three features which contribute to this *diary* style. Find examples of each feature in the passage.

the disabled noted positively, as well as amazement at the irritating habit buses have of arriving *exactly* on time. However, some criticism of television programmes and the fact that supper is always the same – bread, *Wurst* and cheese.

My turn to teach the group. The language skills of boys between 14 and 17 varies considerably. But where are Tom and David? "Gone into town, sir. Visiting their *local*."

Saturday: Relax at the home of the teacher I am staying with, an arrangement that has worked well for the past 10 years. We go to another teacher's house for dinner. I am impressed. A large house with expensive furnishings and a new car. We compare our jobs. I get the impression he is not under as much pressure, with fewer administration worries and more

time to prepare his lessons. His pupils no doubt benefit from it, but I can't help feeling that an afternoon on the games field gives me additional job satisfaction. It is good to spend time with pupils outside the classroom. Still I wish I had his money...

Sunday: Wake to the news that the ground war has started. Doris is full of horror at the wastefulness of it all. Jürgen is more pragmatic. Hope there will be no more phone calls today. Robert has seen the week through. I feel as if I have done as much as I could to help and yet am frustrated by the fact that he will go back having had a miserable stay with a negative picture of life in a German family. Almost all the others seem to have had an enjoyable and profitable stay.

Monday: 8.50am. We meet at the station. All here except Tom. "Are the pubs open, sir?" 8.55am: Tom arrives. Train to Frankfurt airport. Simon goes off to buy a German newspaper with his last few pfennigs. "Can't understand much of this, sir." He has picked up a Turkish paper. Clearly his German has come on in leaps and bounds.

We sit in the plane on the tarmac for an hour for reasons beyond BA's control. Then, Heathrow at last. Exit through customs is suddenly slowed down. "My family gave me some wine to bring back, sir."

As always, on the coach back to school I wonder whether it has all been worthwhile. "Thanks for organising it, sir. Will we be able to go again next year?" There's my answer.

5 Find the following questions in the passage. Do you think the writer really wants an answer?

1 Is it really such a good idea to start school this early?
2 Why is the guide's English so good?
3 What am I doing teaching in England?

Rewrite them saying what he really thinks.

6 Find these words or expressions in the passage and answer the questions.

lad-about-town impression: The boy does not correspond to the description he gave of himself. What do you think his parents are like?
fervour: Are the British or the Germans enthusiastic about the Gulf war?
antipathy: Is this likely to be a positive or a negative attitude?
dismay: Are the English boys as enthusiastic as the Germans?

7 The diary describes the visit from the teacher's point of view. Imagine you are one of the schoolchildren, perhaps Robert, Tom or David. Write a description of the visit from your point of view as a diary entry or as a telephone call which you made home.

3 I can't get rid of the smell of burning

1 In the passage on page 10, which appeared in *The Independent*, the writer, Suzanne Moore, describes a fire she had at her flat. Before you read it, think of three or four situations at home in which a fire can start.

2 Here are the first lines of each paragraph. Put them in the right order and find out how the fire started.

a) I could hear the firemen crashing about and shouting.

b) And now, a few days later, I am starting to feel very strange.

c) It started under the grill.

d) We could hear the sirens of the fire engines.

e) I arrived with two kids and bags full of smelly clothes in a taxi.

f) The firemen were back. "Let's take you in there to have a look."

g) I phoned a friend.

h) Returning to my "new home", my daughter presented me with a picture she had drawn.

i) By now flames were coming out of the top of the cooker.

j) A minute later, smoke was pouring out of all the windows of my flat.

Now read the passage and check.

3 The writer tends to imply things rather than state them directly. What words or phrases would you use to describe the reactions of the following people?

the people in the street
her next-door neighbour
the firemen
an old lady
her neighbour's girlfriend
her friend's son
her friend

I can't get rid of the smell of burning

IT STARTED under the grill. I could smell something burning, so I turned it off. The phone rang. I picked it up: "Janet, I can't talk to you now – something is on fire in my kitchen."

By now flames were coming out of the top of the cooker. Thick black smoke was pouring out from somewhere. Within about 30 seconds, I could see a small fire was turning into a blaze. I needed help. I rushed over the road to my local shop and they called the fire brigade.

A minute later, smoke was pouring out of all the windows of my flat. People in the street were stopping to look. Ray, my next-door neighbour, was just coming home. He saw what was happening and rushed in to try to close the door. He came out choking, sweat dripping down his face, his hair singed. "Shit, it's hot in there, man." Everyone was shouting at me: "Where are the kids? Are they in there?" "They're at school, it's all right." But it wasn't all right – my flat was on fire. I could see the flames licking up the kitchen window. I started crying – a coat around my shoulders.

We could hear the sirens of the fire engines. Four of them arrived together. About three minutes after we had called them. One fireman was down on his stomach, slithering in under the smoke, into the kitchen. I don't know how he did it. Every human instinct tells you to get away from fire. And yet these men were doing just the opposite. For a job that pays comparatively little. For a job that sometimes kills them. I could hear breaking glass. "That's your windows gone, girl," said an old lady who seemed to be enjoying the whole thing. "Come and sit down next door." Ray's girlfriend was making me tea. Ray was offering me vodka. "Sit by the fire," he offered. "You need warming up."

I could hear the firemen crashing about and shouting. Jesus, my house was burning down, and there was nothing I could do. One of the firemen came in, huge, in huge boots. "Is that your flat, love? You don't want to go in there yet. Just wait a while." A couple of people from the council appeared. Someone stuck a leaflet in my hand on how to prevent fires. Everyone was asking me questions. "Where are you going to stay?" "Do you want us to put you in bed and breakfast?" No, no, I didn't want that. "Do you want to phone someone up?" Yes, I did, but to say what? Can I live with you? Besides, I couldn't remember a single phone number.

The firemen were back. "Let's take you in there to have a look." Sweet black smoke still hung in the air. There was no electricity. My hall was covered in black debris. My kitchen was just kind of gone: the cooker, the fridge, the washing-machine gutted. Bits from the ceiling, cables and casing were hanging down, twisted by the heat. The ceiling was in fragments by the door. Everything was soaking wet. It stank. "It could have been worse," said the fireman, a phrase I have heard a lot in the last few days. I thanked him for getting there so quickly. "We're not the police, you know," he laughed. Then I apologised for having started a fire in the first place. "It's our job," he said. "Just like *London's Burning*."

And off they went.

I phoned a friend. She was at work, but her 11-year-old son, Oliver, was there. "There's been a fire, um, can we come and stay?" "A fire? Wow, great. Yeah, see yer."

I arrived with two kids and bags full of smelly clothes in a taxi. My friend spent the weekend feeding me, giving me very large gin and tonics and telling me that everything would be all right. We went back to the flat to examine the devastation. Some things appeared almost untouched, such as the bag of apples I bought the day before. The clock on the wall had melted into something out of a Dali painting, but it was still working. Everything was covered in a layer of thick black dust.

And now, a few days later, I am starting to feel very strange. Very, very tired and slightly dislocated. One day I had a flat, the next day I didn't. I had become a sort of refugee. Then I see pictures of Yugoslavia and feel silly for saying that. I have only lost a kitchen, these people have lost everything. I try to cheer myself up by thinking that I will be getting what every girl wants for Christmas – a lot of new shiny kitchen appliances. Or so I have been told by the insurance company who came and inspected the damage. "It could have been worse," they said.

Returning to my "new home", my daughter presented me with a picture she had drawn. "To Mummy, love from Scarlet." It was a picture of a house on fire. I had to laugh. But as I was laughing I caught that smell again. I just can't seem to get rid of it. Everywhere I go, I can smell something burning.

4 Look for the point in the passage when she comments directly on her own reactions. Would you describe the overall style as calm or emotional?

Another aspect of the passage's style is the large number of short sentences and the absence of linking words like *and* and *but* while she is describing the events of the fire itself. What effect do you think this has?

There are some words and phrases which reveal her feelings while her home was on fire.

> I <u>rushed</u> over the road ...
> But <u>it wasn't all right</u> – my flat
> was on fire.

Can you find other words or phrases which reveal her feelings?

5 Answer the questions about vocabulary. Use a dictionary to help you, if necessary.

1 'He came out *choking* . . .' If smoke was pouring out of the flat, what effect would this have on someone who went in?
2 '. . . his hair *singed*.' There were flames in the flat. His skin wasn't burnt, but what are the flames likely to do to his hair?
3 '. . . the cooker, the fridge, the washing-machine *gutted*.' What is likely to be left of these household appliances after a fire?
4 'Very, very tired and slightly *dislocated*.' Physically, she felt tired. How do you think she felt emotionally?

6 Answer the questions.

1 '"Sit by the fire," he offered. "You need warming up."' What is the irony in her neighbour's remark?
2 '"We're not the police, you know," he laughed.' What might the fireman be implying about the police?
3 '"It could have been worse," said the fireman, a phrase I have heard a lot in the last few days.' How much worse could it have been? Do you think the writer is comforted by this remark?

7 Write some advice on what you should do when a fire starts.

Now use your notes to write the leaflet that the people from the council gave the writer.

4 | Imperial English

1 In the article below, which appeared in *Scientific American*, Professor Anne Eisenberg writes about the importance of English in the scientific world. For which jobs or subjects is it important to know English in your country?

2 The statements below express the main idea of each paragraph. Read the article and match the statements to the paragraphs.

a) In many countries English is now a practical second language.
b) Meetings were often held in several languages.
c) Most resistance to English has disappeared.
d) Americans may be changing their attitude to learning foreign languages.
e) Unlike Heisenberg, most American science students only speak English.
f) After World War II the USA became the international leader in science and technology.
g) English may survive longer than American scientific leadership just as Latin survived longer than the Roman Empire.
h) American scientists have not needed to learn other languages for the last few decades.
i) Some countries resisted the linguistic dominance of English.
j) Before World War II scientists had to learn foreign languages in order to understand scientific publications.

Decide which sentences in each paragraph express the main ideas.

Imperial English: The Language of Science?

WERNER HEISENBERG learned Latin, Greek and French when he was a gymnasium student in Munich. Later, when he worked in Copenhagen, he tackled English and Danish, using mealtimes as his language lab: English conversation during breakfast; Danish read aloud from the newspaper by his landlady afterward. This is not the kind of anecdote we associate with today's science majors in the US, that resolutely monolingual lot. Science students here are rarely to be found in a school language lab, much less a spontaneous one, and when they do speak another language, it is usually because of family background, not classroom instruction. Then they graduate, attend a conference with colleagues from other countries and discover the international hallmark of US science: linguistic incompetence.

We are the people who can no longer be bothered to learn another language. To be sure, we really haven't had to since the 1960s, for in the

12

years since World War II English has gradually but inexorably become the *lingua franca* of science. Today it is the universal currency of international publications as well as of meetings. Those of us who need to keep up with, say, *Angewandte Chemie* need not worry about mastering German; we can leave it to the journal's staff, whose English is no doubt immaculate, to provide us with a convenient international edition published, of course, in English.

It wasn't always this way. For the 200 years before World War II, most scientific work was reported in German, French or English, in that order of importance. People who wanted to keep up with a specialization had to learn the dominant language of the field. For example, scientists who wished to understand quantum mechanics in the 1920s had to learn German. Sir Nevill Mott comments, "Apart from Dirac, I don't think anyone in Cambridge understood (quantum mechanics) very well; there were no lectures on it, and so the only thing to do was to learn German and read the original papers, particularly those of Schrödinger and Born's *Wellenmechanik der Stossvorgänge* ('Wave Mechanics of Collision Processes')."

German, French and English were the customary languages of meetings, too. At Niels Bohr's institute in Copenhagen, for example, John A. Wheeler recalls that most seminars were held in German, occasionally in English. Bohr, who spoke English and German with equal ease, fluctuated between them, adding Danish as counterpoint. No one had to learn French, though, for Bohr's knowledge of it was limited. "I have it from an eyewitness," Abraham Pais writes, "that he once greeted the French ambassador to Denmark with a cordial *aujourd'hui*."

After World War II, the linguistic balance of power shifted. The US economy boomed, and science grew rapidly as vast federal expenditure, often fueled by the cold war, poured into research and development. US scientists flocked to conferences, bringing their language with them; US scientific publications burgeoned, and their huge readerships made them highly desirable to scientists throughout the world who realized English was a medium through which they could be widely read and cited.

With technical dominance came the beginning of linguistic dominance, first in Europe, then globally. Only the French and the Soviets put up a spirited resistance. At one international conference when de Gaulle was still in power, for instance, a member of the French contingent began reporting in French and then, sensing that many of the important US scientists in his audience did not understand him, switched to English. Then he watched as all of his French colleagues rose as a group and exited. The Soviets, too, did what they could to fight the English monopoly, providing expensive simultaneous technical translations and bilingual commentaries or even resorting to French as the lesser evil – anything to avoid the language of the enemy.

Today in the former USSR, linguistic opposition has dissolved with the union. Even the French, who fiercely cherish their language, have accepted the practicality of English for publishing the proceedings of international meetings: the 12th Colloquium on High Resolution Molecular Spectroscopy was held last year in Dijon, but the only speech in French during the five days of the meeting was the mayor's welcoming address.

The rest of the world's scientists, too, have fallen into step. English was already in place in India, Nigeria and many other countries where it had been left behind by the British, to be widely adopted as a practical second language that united diverse populations. The Japanese readily inserted the language of the victor into their children's school programs; Korean and Chinese scientists were delighted to take up membership in the English-speaking club.

English is indeed the new Latin. It has become a successor to the scholarly language once so powerful that Christian Huygens delayed publishing *Traité de la Lumière* for 12 years in hopes of translating it into Latin so as "to obtain greater attention to the thing". And there is a second way that English may parallel Latin. Latin outlived the Roman Empire, surviving long after the government that spread it through the world had vanished. So may the international use of English outlast US scientific domination. The ascent of English, after all, had little to do with any inherent linguistic virtues. True, English has an unusually rich vocabulary; instead of resisting new terms, we welcome them, particularly in science and technology – *les anglicismes* have conquered the world. But it was scientific leadership, not a flexible lexicon, that sparked the diffusion of English. Many now say this leadership is faltering. Consider, for instance, last year's top holders of new US patents: Toshiba, Mitsubishi and Hitachi.

This year, although English continues its reign, small changes are in the wind. For example, more than 860 Japanese language programs are running in US schools, and there is even an occasional undergraduate science department promoting German. Who knows, the students enrolling in these foreign language classes might even learn a bit more about English, or, to put it in Goethe's words, *Wer fremde Sprachen nicht kennt, weiss nichts von seiner eigenen.*

Anne Eisenberg is a professor at Polytechnic University in Brooklyn, where a very popular Japanese language course was recently begun.

3

In each of these sentences from the article there is a word missing. Without looking back at the passage, try to complete the sentences with these alternative words or phrases. There are three extra words.

weakening   delegation   difficult   changed   love dearly
stereotype   characteristic   finished   perfect
increased in number

1 Then they (American science students) graduate, attend a conference with colleagues from other countries and discover the international .... of US science: linguistic incompetence.

2 ... we can leave it to the journal's staff, whose English is no doubt ...., to provide us with a convenient international edition published, of course, in English.

3 After World War II, the linguistic balance of power ....

4 US scientific publications ...., and their huge readerships made them highly desirable to scientists throughout the world ...

5 At one international conference (...) a member of the French .... began reporting in French ...

6 Even the French, who fiercely .... their language, have accepted the practicality of English for publishing the proceedings of international meetings ...

7 Many now say this (scientific) leadership is ....

Look back at the article and find out what the missing words are.

4

Look at this extract.

> ... when he worked in Copenhagen, he tackled English and Danish, using mealtimes as his language lab: English conversation during breakfast; Danish read aloud from the newspaper by his landlady afterward.

The writer is suggesting that Heisenberg worked hard to learn foreign languages. What is she suggesting in the following sentences?

1 "...he once greeted the French ambassador to Denmark with a cordial *aujourd'hui.*"

2 ... all of his French colleagues rose as a group and exited.

3 ... Christian Huygens delayed publishing *Traité de la Lumière* for 12 years in hopes of translating it into Latin so as "to obtain greater attention to the thing".

4 Consider, for instance, last year's top holders of new US patents: Toshiba, Mitsubishi and Hitachi.

5 How does the writer feel about her compatriots' linguistic incompetence? ⚷
Can you find words or expressions which reveal her opinion?

6 What, according to the writer, is the reason for the linguistic dominance of ⚷
English in the scientific world? Do you agree with her analysis? Would you
say that this is also true for other disciplines or jobs that you thought about
in Exercise 1?

7 What is the general attitude in your country to the international diffusion of
English? Would you say that people:

– resist it?
– accept it reluctantly?
– accept it willingly?

5 | Just another Saturday as a sheep in wolves' clothing

1 Have you ever been to a football match? Are you a football fan? If so, what team do you support? Do you go to all their matches? What do you enjoy about football matches? If not, why do you think so many people go to football matches?

Why do you think football generates violence in some countries? Are supporters violent in your country?

Just another Saturday as a sheep in wolves' clothing

FIFTEEN minutes to kick-off. The streets around the stadium are empty except for policemen standing on corners, watching for trouble. The fans are all inside, taunting each other with massed chants. You can't hear the words at this distance, but the tone is clear: harsh, guttural, rising in excitement, the noise amplified by the stadium roof. A police helicopter passes low overhead.

As we approach the ground, my friend and I have one final negotiation to make. He is a Wolverhampton Wanderers fan. I support the home team, Brighton. It is my local team. But there is no neutral place to stand – we must watch the match among my people or his. "Let's go in with the Wolves." I say, conceding; he is my guest. "Thanks," he says. "I appreciate it."

By standing together, though, we are breaking the rules. All the entrances to the stadium are marked either "Home Supporters Only" or "Away Supporters Only". Each entrance is guarded by a small group of policemen. We walk along the side of the stadium, looking for a viable turnstile. The police question us as we walk past. "You're Wolves, are you?" they say. "Right. Along there." I nod, having to lie.

As we approach a turnstile, we are both taken to the wall and given a routine body-search. The officer searches my body for weapons, first bending down and clutching at my ankles, then moving his hands upwards stiffly, squeezing my thighs, my crotch, my hips, pressing the flat of his hand down my sides, across my pockets. If he were to take my wallet out of my pocket and find my address, we would be faced with an awkward situation.

Now we are inside the Wolverhampton enclosure, penned into a section of the stadium by thick wire fences, patrolled by police on all sides. Before we can get a view of the pitch we must cross another cordon of police. "Go down there, on the right, towards the front," we are told. "Down on the right. It's too congested on the left."

We pass down the central aisle. The crowd on either side is thick, jammed against the crash barriers, swaying. They are chanting and punching the air in unison.

Wolves have a good turnout at away matches; we duck down, under the metal barriers, surfacing a moment later in a group of suedeheads who are all wearing old-gold Wolves shirts. The noise is muffled until you get above shoulder level. Then you can hear it. The abuse is loud, untethered; these young men are shaking with rage. The man next to me is shouting obscenities. He has a wolf's head, the Wolverhampton club crest, tattooed on his arm. His old-gold shirt is tied around his waist. He looks me straight in the face and wipes his mouth, which is dribbling slightly, on the back of his hand.

It is impossible for me to show any sign that I

16

> 'Some people think football is a matter of life and death... I can assure you it is more serious than that.'
>
> Bill Shankly, football manager

2 In the passage, the writer, William Leith, describes a football match he went to in England. Before you read it, think of words or phrases which you associate with the following:

fan   police   team   match   referee   stadium

3 There is a play on words in the title of the passage. Read the passage and decide what it is. Who are the sheep and the wolves?

8 support my own team. In fact, to pass muster I must demonstrate the opposite. When a chant starts, I must join in, punching the air. When a refereeing decision, even a fair one, goes against Wolverhampton, I must scowl and curse.

9 Another development: my friend, Nigel, an English PhD, is as enthusiastic as the rest of them. He knows all the songs. I hadn't noticed up to this point, but he's wearing an old-gold shirt. My shirt is black. At least that's the colour of the Wolverhampton shorts. Nigel has a great line in abusing the referee. He screams: "Milford, you ****, what kind of hairstyle is that?" The suedeheads around us snicker their approval.

10 Halfway through the second half, Wolves take the lead. A superb move wrong-foots the defence, leaving Andy Mutch with an open shot at goal. He scores. My heart sinks; my team are down. The men I am jammed against leap into the air, screaming as loudly as they can, punching the air, turning and pushing each other. I must follow them. I scream and shout. Someone has his arm around me; someone else is shaking his fist in my face, his mouth half open, yelling and yelling.

11 Football supporters have a rigid code of behaviour on the terraces. The next phase of the proceedings is to stand, both arms raised in the air, and sing the name of the scorer while clapping. We put our arms up, and I find myself, awkwardly, starting to sing.

It is more difficult to disguise your joy when your own team scores than to feign it when the opposition does. But the code is rigid on all points. A decision against you, a foul or an offside, means that the referee is either stupid or biased. When your team is penalised for fouling, you scream *"Never!"* When your team fouls and gets away with it, you laugh. When the opposition misses a goal, you turn to its supporters and taunt them with obscene gestures. And when the opposition scores, you are silent, pretending not to have noticed. For 90 minutes you abandon 12 logic. An interesting thing happens when you do this. The mood of the crowd with its canned anger, its hysteria, its panic, begins to take you over, to enter your consciousness. You can't fight it. As the game progresses, I feel my allegiance being shifted. When all logic has disappeared, something else – a bit of panic, a bit of hysteria – rushes in to replace it. When Steve Bull, the Wolves centre-forward, has the ball in front of goal, I feel vaguely titillated by the hope that he will score. When he does, my happiness is not entirely counterfeit.

The final score is 3–3, Brighton scoring the equaliser 10 minutes from the end. This means that the Wolves fans, feeling robbed of victory, are the most likely to start fights after the match. But vicious fights are rare now; the police choreograph the movements of the fans after the match with precision. After the final whistle, we 13 are locked in while the home supporters are escorted away. We emerge into the sunny streets, cursing gently. No fights break out. Screaming abuse for 90 minutes is enough for most people. The police smile at us as we walk past. This has been no more than an ordinary Saturday afternoon.

4 Read the passage again and answer the questions.

1 The writer is faced with a dilemma before entering the football stadium. Which sentences make this dilemma clear?
2 Why is this such a problem and what effect does it have on his subsequent behaviour?
3 What surprising discovery does he make about his own feelings towards the end of the match?

Do you think the writer would choose the same word and phrase associations as you did in Exercise 2?

5 The writer sometimes implies ideas rather than stating them explicitly. What is he suggesting in the sentences below?

1 'By standing together, though, we are breaking the rules.'   What rules?
2 'Wolves have a good turnout at away matches.'   How many Wolves' supporters are there at the match?
3 'Another development: my friend, Nigel, *an English PhD*, is as enthusiastic as the rest of them.'   What is the purpose of the words *in italics*?
4 'As the game progresses, I feel my allegiance being shifted.'   What allegiance is he referring to? What does the choice of words suggest about his responsibility in the change?

6 Find these words in the passage and choose the correct meaning in the context.

conceding (paragraph 2)	a) refusing b) giving in c) accepting
congested (paragraph 5)	a) dangerous b) uncomfortable c) overcrowded
untethered (paragraph 7)	a) unrestrained b) unlimited c) unbelievable
feign (paragraph 12)	a) pretend b) simulate c) imagine
canned (paragraph 12)	a) instant b) excessive c) tinned
counterfeit (paragraph 12)	a) false b) real c) imagined
choreograph (paragraph 13)	a) organise b) practise c) watch

18

7 **Answer the questions about the writer's style.**

1 In the first paragraph the writer creates the atmosphere of the match.
How would you describe this atmosphere? Which words or expressions
are particularly effective?

2 What is the main verb tense used in the passage? What effect does this
have on the tone of the passage?

3 'The man next to me is shouting obscenities . . . and wipes his mouth,
which is dribbling slightly, on the back of his hand.'   What impression of
the fans does the writer convey?

8 **Look through the passage again and write down some words or phrases
which the writer associates with the words in Exercise 2.**

9 **The writer says that his logic disappears and his allegiance shifts during the
match. What do you think happens when his logic returns after the match?
What does this suggest about the real nature of this kind of allegiance?**

**Have you ever experienced anything similar? What implications could this
have in other areas of life? Think about things you believe in passionately,
and then think about the possible circumstances in which your feelings might
change.**

6 | We've never had it so bad

1   The article in this unit is about teenagers in the 1990s. It was written by a British writer, Caitlin Moran, when she was sixteen. Do you think a teenager today could say 'We've never had it so bad'? Think about what a teenager in your country might complain about.

2   Read the article and find out if it mentions any of the ideas you thought about in Exercise 1.

3   Choose five words or phrases from the following list which seem to summarise the general meaning of the article.

       material world   drugs   cry   vote   sell   self-loathing
       misery   protest marches   angst   symbols   identity   future
       art gallery   parents' generation   nothing   depressing   mirror
       middle-class   clothes   war   rebellion   advertisers

Without looking back at the passage, write five sentences using the words you chose. Try and convey the main ideas of the article.

4   What evidence can you find for the following statements?

1   The writer's friend hates life because she is still too young to do things without her parents' permission.
2   She is happy to accept the identity the advertisers sell her.
3   The Nineties' teenage cult is self-hate rather than rebellion.
4   Drugs are one of the main causes of the teenagers' passive attitude to life.
5   They have adopted another generation's values because they have none of their own.
6   The material comfort and safety of middle-class life does not make a teenager's plight any easier.
7   Protesting and rebelling against parents is better than self-loathing.

20

We've never had it so bad

What's so great about being a teenager in the material world of the Nineties? asks **Caitlin Moran**

WHERE is the anger? Where is the protest? Where is the teenage point of view these days? Where are the rebellions and the cults and the things that adults can't understand?

Why are 'the youth of today' living the 'there's a club ... and you go and you stand on your own, and you leave on your own, and you cry and you want to die' life and still happy to accept it?

One of my friends, at 16 – six and ten years on this planet, four leap years – says that her life terrifies her because, when she looks at it, it seems so long until she'll die. At 16. Welcoming oblivion, when she's too young to vote, too young to drive, too young to leave home without her parents' permission.

She's not on drugs or the mother of an unwanted child, she lives a middle-class existence in a low-crime suburb, and she has no identity except that which advertisers sell her: it is too confining, both physically and mentally.

Sometimes we climb up on to a five-storey car park, and throw bits of gravel at the people below, and she'll shout 'Who am I?' and I laugh till I cry because no one can hear us, and nobody can tell her.

We sit on the steps outside the art gallery and she'll tell me her plan for the future: 'I don't know', and I'll read her palm and make up things, because 'nothing' is too depressing. She reapplies her eyeliner for the fifth time that day, and I gloomily pick nut chips out of a Fruit and Nut block.

She puts her little mirror back in her bag and tells me that she wants to be sick every time she sees her face, and she wouldn't mind giving up her future right to vote if she could live in a country where the women wear veils.

And she hugs the railings and looks like she could melt away at any minute with misery, and what can I say? She saw her face in the mirror, and she's been made to hate it so much that it distorted.

Why the self-loathing?

Why do thousands and thousands of teenagers suddenly hate their picked upon, pressurised selves? Instead of shouting at their parents, which is what parents expect and justify their grey hairs with, why do teenagers shout at themselves? Who's going to stand up for them? Jiminy Cricket?

I'm angry, and I'm scared because no one else seems to be.

I'm angry that there is no 'Nineties' scene. We're being given our parents' music and clothes and angst and I want to know why. Is it because the past isn't dangerous? It's been coped with and poses no threat? What are we afraid of now? Why are we being sold the traumas of the Vietnam war when we had our own war, our own Nineties war, to feel concerned about and go on marches about and have T-shirt slogans about?

We've been sold another generation's problems, symbols and ethics. They look silly and they don't fit.

5 The writer suggests that teenagers are being manipulated into accepting another generation's identity and values. For example:

'. . . she has no identity except that which advertisers sell her . . .'

Can you find other instances of this idea in the article?
What reason does she suggest may be behind this manipulation?
Who do you think the writer is referring to?

6 Look back at the sentences you wrote in Exercise 3. Would you change any of them now you are more familiar with the passage? Use these sentences to write a short summary of the article.

7 Do you agree with Caitlin Moran's analysis of the teenager's plight?

How do or did your experiences as a teenager compare to those described in the article?

Make a list of ideas you could include in an article which is much more optimistic about teenage life today.

7 | In affection and esteem

1 The short story in this unit is by the English author Mary Webb (1888–1927). It is about a woman who has 'an impossible dream'. Can you remember ever dreaming about something you wanted very much indeed? Did your dream become a reality? How did you feel? Is there something you still dream of today?

2 Look at the picture of the main character in this story and imagine:

- where she lives
- who she lives with
- what a typical day in her life is like
- what she does for a living

3 Read the first part of the story. Can you add anything to your answers in Exercise 2?

Miss Myrtle Brown had never received the gift of a box or a bouquet of flowers. She used to think, as she trudged away to the underground station every day, to go and stitch buttonholes in a big London shop, that it would have been nice if, on one of her late returns, she had found a bunch of roses – red, with thick, lustrous petals, deeply sweet, or white, with their rare fragrance – awaiting her on her table. It was, of course, an impossible dream. She ought to be glad enough to have a table at all, and a loaf to put on it. She ought to be grateful to those above for letting her have a roof over her head.

"You might," she apostrophized herself, as she lit her gas ring and put on the kettle, "not *have* a penny for this slot. You might, Myrtle Brown, not *have* a spoonful of tea to put in this pot. Be thankful!"

And she was thankful to Providence, to her landlady, to her employer, who sweated his workers, to the baker for bringing her loaf, to the milkman for leaving her half a pint of milk on Sundays, to the landlady's cat for refraining from drinking it.

Yet she could not help thinking, when she put out her light and lay down, of the wonderful moment if ever she *did* receive a bouquet.

Think of unpacking the box! Think of seeing on the outside, 'Cut Flowers. Immediate', undoing the string, taking off the paper, lifting the lid!

What then? Ah, violets, perhaps, or roses; lilies of the valley, lilac or pale pink peonies or mimosa with its warm sweetness.

The little room would be like a greenhouse – like one of the beautiful greenhouses at Kew. She would borrow jam pots from the landlady, and it would take all evening to arrange them. And the room would be wonderful – like heaven.

To wake, slowly and luxuriously, on a Sunday morning, into that company – what bliss!

She might, of course, out of her weekly wage, buy a bunch of flowers. She did occasionally. But that was not quite the perfect thing, not quite what she desired. The centre of all the wonder was to be the little bit of pasteboard with her name on it, and the sender's name, and perhaps a few words of greeting. She had heard that this was the custom in sending a bouquet to anyone – a great actress or a prima donna. And on birthdays it was customary, and at funerals.

Birthdays! Suppose, now, she received such a parcel on her birthday. She had had so many birthdays, and they had all been so very much alike. A tomato with her tea, perhaps, and a cinema afterwards. Once it had been a pantomime, the landlady having been given a ticket, and having passed it on in consideration of some help with needlework.

4

Decide what evidence, if any, there is in the first part of the passage for these statements.

1 She lived a very lonely life.
2 She worked very hard.
3 Her life was rather tedious.
4 She adored flowers more than anything else.
5 She felt guilty about her *impossible dream.*
6 She was getting old.
7 She wanted to be a great actress or a prima donna.

5

Why does Miss Brown think that boxed flowers would be so much better than ones she has bought for herself? What does this suggest about her life?

6

Miss Brown makes a *reckless decision*. Can you guess what it is?

Read the next part of the story and see if you were right.

Always in her heart was the longing for some great pageant, some splendid gift of radiance. How she would enjoy it! But nobody seemed anxious to inaugurate any pageant. And, at last, on a bleak winter day when everything had gone wrong and she had been quite unable to be grateful to anybody, she made a reckless decision. She would provide a pageant for herself. Before she began to save up for the rainy day, she would save up for the pageant.

"After that," she remarked, carefully putting crumbs on the windowsill for the birds, "you'll be quiet. You'll be truly thankful, Myrtle Brown."

She began to scrimp and save. Week by week the little hoard increased. A halfpenny here and a penny there – it was wonderful how soon she amassed a shilling. So great was her determination that, before her next birthday, she had got together two pounds.

"It's a wild and wicked thing to spend two pounds on what neither feeds nor clothes," she said. She knew it would be impossible to tell the landlady. She would never hear the last of it. No! It must be a dead secret. Nobody must know where those flowers came from. What was the word people used when you were not to know the name? 'Anon'. Yes. The flowers must be 'anon'. There was a little shop at Covent Garden where they would sell retail. Wonderful things were heaped in hampers. She would go there on the day before her birthday.

7 Answer the questions.

1 What is her *reckless decision*?
2 'Always in her heart was the longing for *some great pageant, some splendid gift of radiance.*'   A *pageant* is a very grand and colourful ceremony. How do these images contrast with her present life?
3 How does she feel about her plan?
4 '". . . you'll be quiet. You'll be truly thankful, Myrtle Brown."'   Do you think this is likely to be true?

8 What do you think happens next? Read on and find out.

She was radiant as she surveyed early London from the bus. She descended at Covent Garden, walking through the piled crates of greenstuff, the casks of fruit, the bursting sacks of potatoes. The shopkeeper was busy. He saw a shabby little woman with an expression of mingled rapture and anxiety.

"I want some flowers. Good flowers. They are to be packed and sent to a lady I know, tonight."

"Violets?"

"Yes, violets and tuberoses and lilies and pheasant-eye and maidenhair and mimosa and a few dozen roses."

"Wait a minute! Wait a minute! I suppose you know they'll cost you a pretty penny."

"I can pay for what I order," said Miss Brown with hauteur. "Write down what I say, add it up as you go on, put down box and postage, and I'll pay."

The shopkeeper did as he was told.

Miss Brown went from flower to flower, like a sad-coloured butterfly, softly touching a petal, softly sniffing a rose. The shopkeeper, realizing that something unusual was afoot, gave generous measure. At last the order was complete, the address given, the money – all the two pounds – paid.

"Any card enclosed?" queried the shopman.

Triumphantly Miss Brown produced one. 'In affection and esteem.'

"A good friend, likely?" queried the shopman.

"Almost my only friend," replied Miss Brown.

Through Covent Garden's peculiarly glutinous mud she went in a beatitude, worked in a beatitude, went home in a dream.

9 Can you guess how the story ends? Do you think it is a happy or an unhappy ending? Why?

Turn to page 83 of the *Answer key* and see if you were right.

10 Write a different ending to the story.

8 | Help! I'm turning into my dad

1

How do you like to spend your holidays? With friends or family? In your country, what would be the typical holiday arrangements for a family with young children? Where would they go and what would they do?

2

In the article below, the writer, Jim White, describes his annual family holiday. Look at the following words which come from the article. What do you think he is likely to say about it?

rain   sun   drive   argument   fun   laugh   beach
sightseeing   picnic   ice-cream   embarrass   horror   silence
nerves

The title expresses the main idea of the passage. What do you expect it to be about? What does the title tell us about the writer?

Now read the passage and see if you were right.

Help! I'm turning into my dad

IT WAS raining. On a holiday where you expected to be basking like lizards in the sun all day, there wasn't much else to do except go for a drive. Again. We drove about 60 miles to discover that the glass-blowing demonstration we thought the children might like to see did not take place on Wednesdays.

On the way back my wife took a wrong turning. A dispute about the route developed into an argument that concluded when she turned the car into a shop forecourt and suggested it would be best if I drove.

I snapped the car into reverse and accelerated into a row of ornamental plant pots, spilling begonias and marigolds on to the shop's steps. The owner ran out and we agreed that 100 francs would cover the damage. I didn't have any money. So I had to ask my wife for a sub.

Are family holidays meant to be like this? You don't remember the fun times, you remember the occasion your dad disabled the car by filling it with diesel. You don't remember the laughs on the beach, you remember the endless sightseeing visits to churches that your dad made you do, the wine-tasting trips he made you go to when you were too young to taste any wine, the car-bound picnics your dad organised in castle car parks as the rain fell and the windows steamed up.

You resolved then that you wouldn't let it happen like that when you were a dad, when you called the shots, when it was your turn to organise the holiday. You wouldn't embarrass your children by wearing a Hawaiian shirt in a built-up area, you wouldn't ration them to one ice-cream a day. You wouldn't let some local drunk get one over on you in an argument.

They say that some people who were beaten or sexually abused as youngsters end up inflicting the same horrors on their own children, but as yet nobody has documented other forms of learnt behaviour. Like taking your children on the same holidays your parents treated you to.

It is when you first take your children on such a holiday that a realisation slowly dawns: the ballooning waist and the thinning hair are not symptoms simply of ageing but of a more frightening metamorphosis. You are turning into your father. Or rather, as this condition knows no sexual exclusivity, your father or mother. As you hit your thirties, you realise all the energy you expended in your teens and twenties growing your hair, rebelling, trying to be anything but them was completely wasted.

It is on a family holiday that you notice it first, because that was where we saw most of our dads, were introduced to mannerisms and attitudes that would become our own 25 years later. In those days before New Men, they didn't do many of the nose-blowing, bottom-wiping, potty-training chores of everyday life. Suddenly on holiday there was this unfamiliar figure taking us around obscure French ecclesiastical sights and filling from the wrong petrol pump.

And when you get the holiday snaps back, the grainy, arty, black-and-white shots of yourself bonding with your children look frighteningly similar to the grainy Box Brownie black and whites of dad – his Fifties fashions looking much like today's – cuddling you.

Despite what we might hope, metamorphosis into our parents is not restricted to holiday behaviour. One friend of mine's father used to suggest that when guests came to stay they should bring old clothes. This, the guests imagined, was to equip them for long walks in the woods. But actually they spent their entire stay chopping firewood, rounding up sheep, mending fences, erecting stables, building extensions and saving the host around £10,000 in skilled labour charges.

My friend has adopted this paternal trait wholesale, and now asks dinner party guests to bring a bottle and a Black & Decker.

You can see people turning into their parents all around you. Being famous is no protection. Liza Minnelli increasingly gabbles like Judy Garland, the Prince of Wales holds his hands behind his back just like the old man.

The Hollywood truism is that Michael Douglas is turning into Kirk, though Douglas junior has declined to strip to the waist and swing from the rigging in every film he makes. In Fatal Attraction, one film in which he did slip off his shirt, for a bit of swinging in Glenn Close's rigging, he revealed a midriff that suggested it will require considerable work in the gym if he is to grow as trim as his father.

Back to my own holiday: I had broken the ornamental plant pots, handed over the wheel and we were about 10 minutes down the road when my wife and I broke the silence with a laugh. We decided to stop at a bar – to settle the children's nerves, you understand.

After the drink, I eased the car into a side road and saw a battered red Peugeot pick-up coming down the wrong side of the road. I applied my brakes, but the truck's driver preferred to use the front of our car to bring his vehicle to a halt. I jumped out, he sat where he was. An old peasant, cataracts the size of golf balls, reeking of Pernod, he informed me it was my fault. Five minutes' argument failed to persuade him it was his.

I had let some old French drunk get away with rearranging my radiator. A strong, bloody-minded young man would never have allowed that to happen. But I was just a dad on holiday who had taken the kids to a glass-blowing demonstration on the wrong day.

3 Which of these statements best summarises the main idea of the article?

a) Family holidays are usually a disaster.
b) Children inevitably end up looking and behaving like their parents.
c) We always remember bad times and forget good times.
d) Parents like to take their families on the same sort of holidays they were taken on as children.
e) Famous people grow up to be like their parents.

4 Answer the questions.

1 'It is when you first take your children on such a holiday that a realisation slowly dawns: . . .'   What sort of holiday? What do you realise?
2 What, according to the writer, are 'New Men'? Why do you think they are 'new'?
3 What does the word 'Help!' in the title suggest about the writer's attitude? What other expressions or sentences express this attitude?

5 In each of these sentences from the article there is a word or an expression missing. Without looking back at the article, try and find suitable words to fill the blanks.

1 On a holiday where you expected to be .... like lizards in the sun all day ...

2 I .... the car into reverse and accelerated into a row of ornamental plant pots ...

3 You don't remember the fun times, you remember the occasion your dad .... the car by filling it with diesel.

4 You wouldn't let some local drunk .... in an argument.

5 You .... then that you wouldn't let it happen like that when you were a dad, when you ...., ...

6 My friend has adopted this paternal trait ...., and now asks dinner party guests to bring a bottle and a Black & Decker.

7 When he took off his shirt, Michael Douglas revealed a .... that suggested it will require considerable work in the gym if he is to grow as .... as his father.

Now look at the article again. Did you choose the same words? Do you understand the words in the passage? You can use your dictionary to check.

6   **Match the verbs on the left with their meanings in the context of the passage.**

bask (paragraph 1)	talk
call the shots (paragraph 5)	lie
get one over (paragraph 5)	turn slowly
gabble (paragraph 12)	be in charge
ease (paragraph 15)	damage
rearrange (paragraph 16)	score a point

7   **Read the passage again and make a list of all the words and phrases you can use to describe:**

driving   relationships between parents and children
holiday activities

8   **The style of the article is intended to be humorous, and the humour comes either from ridiculous contrasts or from the unexpected, such as the wine-tasting trips for children too young to drink and the glass-blowing demonstration being closed. Can you find more examples of these in the text? Do you find them humorous?**

9   **Are you like your father/mother? In what ways? Does this bother you? Do you think it is inevitable that we eventually look and behave like our parents?**

Make a list of the qualities you admire in your parents. Have you inherited them?

9 | True stories

1 The newspaper articles in this unit contain a lot of social and cultural information both about the people and the situations described in them, and about the writer.

Read the articles and decide which one you find most amusing, surprising, strange or shocking.

2 Read the articles again. Which of the following is the cause of the incident each one describes? Some may have more than one cause.

a) stupidity or human error
b) legal prohibition
c) culture clash
d) intolerance

e) greed
f) lack of money
g) eccentricity
h) a desire to inflict punishment

3 Each article reveals some social or cultural information about the people and places it describes. For example, in article 1, we learn that there is a Ryzhsky Market in Moscow, and we can infer that a middle-aged man is being very enterprising by selling burnt-out light bulbs. Write sentences describing any social or cultural information you can find or infer in the other articles.

4 The articles also reveal something about the social and cultural background of the writer and of the newspaper that published them. For the articles to be worth publishing, they have to show strange or unexpected behaviour, attitudes or customs. Look at the articles again and decide what would be normal and expected behaviour in the writer's culture. For example, the writer of article 1 doesn't expect people in her own culture to sell burnt-out light bulbs.

1 In Moscow's Ryzhsky Market recently a middle-aged man was doing a brisk business selling burnt-out light bulbs for a rouble each. "Take one of these to work, unscrew a good bulb, put this one in its place, and take the good one home," he advised.

2 Eric Graham of Florida is seeking $10,000 damages in an action against his hairdresser over a haircut which he says was so bad that he needed psychiatric help to overcome the ensuing panic-anxiety disorder.

3 The Irish army's budget is so low that reserve soldiers have to shout "bang! bang!" on exercises because they have no live ammunition and morale was very low, Madeleine Taylor-Quinn, an opposition deputy told parliament in Dublin.

4 **Sardinia:** Maria Viola, 52, had a rapid return to a Cagliari hospital when doctors plastered the wrong foot after she fell and broke her left ankle. She later returned in the same ambulance to get them to rectify the mistake. "I tried to tell them but they said they knew best."

5 **Spotorno:** A judge has rejected claims by a holidaymaker from Milan that the dawn crowing of a rooster near his accommodation in the Italian Riviera resort was unbearable. Police had checked the decibel level of the bird and reported that it did not exceed permitted limits.

6 **Kaikohe** (AP) – Santa Claus, alias John Field, was handing out sweets during the annual parade marking the start of the Christmas season when he ran out of sweets and balloons in the town of Kaikohe on New Zealand's North Island. The children turned nasty and began swearing and kicking at him and calling him a "mean old bastard".

7 Police in Lignano, Italy, were summoned to the beach by outraged bathers who objected to ten middle-aged men playing football in the nude. The whole team has been charged with "indecent acts". Arresting officers were surprised to find the captain was Lignano's chief of police.

8 A passionate Peruvian boyfriend has been arrested and jailed for 24 hours for kissing his fiancée. The embrace occurred on the fourth floor stairwell inside Peru's Palace of Justice in Lima. The man was accused of not showing the building proper respect.

9 A dealer driven to despair by the sound of a musical box on a neighbouring stall at an antiques fair at Great Broughton, North Yorkshire, bought the box for £5 and then smashed it to pieces.

5 The next article is by Tim Jackson, an English journalist for *The Independent*, who lives in Japan. Read it and note the two main things which he finds strange or different from his cultural background.

TOKYO – Ryoanji is the most famous garden in Japan. Yet it contains no trees, no shrubs, no flowers, no fountains – not even a blade of grass. It consists of a small courtyard filled with carefully raked gravel and bordered by a richly weathered wall. In the gravel, apparently at random, sit 15 delicately arranged rocks, some of them slightly covered in moss.

This is the Zen garden, vintage 1499: a garden that has been reduced to its essentials, namely an enclosed space whose minimalism liberates the viewer to contemplate the infinite.

As I sat in the garden's pavilion last Monday, however, it was remarkably difficult to contemplate anything. Behind my right ear was a uniformed tour guide, yelling in exceptionally polite Japanese the dimensions of the garden and the details of how its wall was constructed.

Behind my left ear, a loudspeaker blasted out every seven minutes a recorded potted history, ending with the suggestion that the listener should now peacefully enjoy the garden.

And behind my back, just audible above the bustle of 500 tourists crammed into a small space, the voice of a second tour guide kindly requested ladies and gentlemen from bus number 4 to please make their way to the car park.

The loudspeaker is to be found not just on trains and subways but on buses, too. In most Japanese cities, loudspeakers peal soft music at 5pm to remind children to stop playing and go home. Even cinemas use megaphones to tell their customers that Screen One is full and the film in Screen Two starts in a few minutes.

Yet the ubiquity of noise is a clue to something deep in the Japanese psyche. To a degree that would be unacceptable in Europe or America, people here put up with being told what to do.

At my local underground station, a lady stands on the crossing in front of the entrance, using a whistle to regulate the flow of pedestrians into the station. Police use not only sirens but also voice loudspeakers to order their way through traffic jams. Up and down the country, uniformed men appear as if from nowhere with whistles and flags telling people to stop, walk, go.

Anyone who wants a clue to why Japan is so good at mass production need only go to the Marunouchi line platform of Shinjuku station at 8.30 on a Monday morning, where passengers in neat lines are drilled like cadets by the station staff, kept out of the way of disembarking passengers and then smoothly ushered onto the trains.

The scene is one of tremendous noise and movement. But it gets the passengers on the trains safely much faster than in London. And why does Japan Airlines have such a superb record for punctuality? Partly, at least, because its customers do what they are told.

Yet deep down, few Japanese really seem to like being ordered around. And millions of Japanese have found a way to cut themselves off from the intrusions of authority: the personal stereo. Is it any wonder that the Walkman was invented in Japan?

6 Write down any words or phrases which imply *noise* and *discipline*. For example:

noise: yelling, blasted, . . .
discipline: uniformed, . . .

7 There are many details about the writer's background which we can infer from the passage. For example, if he finds it strange that there are loudspeakers on buses, we can infer that there aren't any in his culture. Note down as many details like this as possible.

8 Read this last article. What do you find surprising or shocking about it?

Customers at the Everglades Bar, in Fort Lauderdale, Florida have taken to livening up their tequilas, peppermint schnapps or Grand Marniers with live wriggling goldfish. Mike Sill, the bar's manager, says the practice began as a joke about a year ago but now the Everglades gets through about *12 dozen* goldfish a month.

10 | Friendship

1 **The passage in this unit is about friendship. Before you read it decide which of the following statements you agree or disagree with.**

a) You can have a lot of friends but only one best friend.
b) Really good friends are always of the same sex.
c) Childhood friendship rarely lasts into adulthood.
d) Time and distance cannot alter real friendship.
e) A friend is someone you can talk freely to.
f) A really good friend is someone with whom you have shared many experiences.
g) Adult friendship is of a different nature from childhood friendship.
h) Childhood friendship is often more emotional than adult friendship.

2 **The following article is about Raymond Blanc, a well-known chef. Read it and decide which statement(s) in Exercise 1 he would agree with.**

I thought the world was caving in, for the first time ever I lost somebody I loved; he didn't die, he just went away, but I still measure all pain by the hurt René caused me.

It was a very nice childhood, an adolescence most people would wish to have, we were living in a tiny village and were a close family, very pleasant, very earthed, and the table was very important.

Our neighbours had a son, and my wonderful childhood was shared with René; basically, we grew up together, we spent every day together, went to school together, we did all the things that children can do. It was a childhood spent in the woods, discovering the beautiful seasons, there was an abundance of produce that grew in the wild, and we went mushrooming and frog hunting, and we searched for *cèpes* under a full moon in winter, which we would sell because my parents didn't have much money.

The adventures that children go through in the making of a friendship, building a tree house and spending a night in the forest – and losing our way back home, these things create a fantastic fabric to the friendship. There was the loving element, too, he was very caring. René was a tall bloke and very strong, and he would be my defender; if anyone ever teased me, he would be there.

It was the finest friendship anyone could have, a brilliant, pure friendship in which you would give your life for your friend.

And life seemed marvellous, it seemed full of sunshine, full of incredible, beautiful things to discover, and I looked forward so much to growing up with René.

And then at the age of 14, his parents moved to the south of France, and we were in the east of France, which is 750 kilometres away ... the south of France sounded like the end of the world.

Well, our parents realised it would be very traumatic, and they did not know how to break the news, so they just announced it the day before. It was a beautiful summer's day, around five o'clock in the evening, and both parents came and said: "We are moving away, and obviously René will have to come with us."

I went quiet for the news to sink in; at first it was sheer disbelief, numbness. I couldn't sleep, and then in the night I understood the impact of the news, I understood that my life would be totally separate from his, and I had to be by myself, alone.

And at that time my world stopped, it was the most incredible pain I have ever experienced, I couldn't see life without my friend, my whole system, my life, was based on René, our friendship was my *life*.

And although he was only going away, he did not die, it was the worst loss I have ever had in my life, still, now, and thirty years later I have not received another shock of that nature.

I had other friends, but never did I achieve that kind of closeness. My world completely collapsed, and nothing was the same, people, the classroom, nature, the country, butterflies.

Maybe because he was more mature he understood a bit better that this was part of life, that life brings people together and separates them, and distance is not necessarily the end.

He accepted that life would separate us, he didn't see it as something final, it was my dramatic side to see only the negative side, self-pity in a way. He is now living a happy life in Provence with a beautiful wife and two lovely daughters, and he is coming here next year, so it is going to be quite wonderful. It is the first time he has ever come to England, he's a good Frenchman, he does not speak a word of English.

Hopefully, we will see each other more, but it is not essential. We now have a beautifully matured, adult friendship where it is easy to talk about anything because we feel totally at ease. There is not a single bitter note, there are no power games, there is nothing secret, there is nothing which detracts from the purity of it.

It is a good, solid relationship that has been established over so many years, and has overcome all the barriers which life and time can create.

I don't think it really could have lasted the way it was.

3 Find these words and expressions in the passage and answer the questions.

1 'I thought the world *was caving in* . . .' Is this likely to be a pleasant or an unpleasant feeling? Can you find another expression in the article which means more or less the same thing?

2 'René was a tall *bloke* . . .' A bloke is a familiar term for a man or a male teenager. Is it likely to be a neutral term or an offensive one?

3 '. . . if anyone ever teased me . . .' When people, particularly children, know each other well, they tease each other. In this context, is this likely to be kind or unkind behaviour?

4 '. . . it would be very traumatic . . .' What would be traumatic? Is this likely to be a pleasant event or a shocking one?

5 '. . . for the news *to sink in* . . .' Choose the best definition for the words *in italics*:
   a) to go deep   b) to be understood   c) to go down

4 The writer uses some very different words to describe his friendship before René's departure and after. For example:

before: beautiful, abundance, full moon, . . .
after: caving in, pain, hurt, . . .

Find more words in the passage to add to the *before* and *after* lists.

5 Think about the relationship and the separation from René's point of view. Which of the words you wrote in Exercise 4 do you think he would use? Write a few sentences describing what happened from his point of view.

How would you describe the parents' reaction to what happened? Would they have used any of the words in Exercise 4?

6 Think of some more questions you would like to ask Raymond Blanc about his friendship with René, or note anything which surprises you about the relationship.

7

Compare your childhood with the writer's. Did you have a very close friend like René?

Write down three names: a childhood friend you still know, a friend with whom you've lost touch and a close friend now. How similar or different are your relationships with each one? Write down some words and phrases to describe these relationships.

11 | New face of ageism

1   This unit is about stereotyped images of old people. Look at the following words and decide which ones you would naturally associate with old age.

     grandparents   sufferer   walking-frame   aerobics   safari
     marathon   denim   crimplene   feminist   disabled
     glamorous   athletic

   Now think of the oldest person you know. Write down words to describe them.

2   Look at the photos. Which words in your list in Exercise 1 would you use to describe them? What different images of old people do the photos represent?

3 In the passage below the writer analyses and comments on past and present stereotypes of old people. Read the first paragraph and decide how the writer would describe the three people in the photos.

New face of ageism

Growing old has not got any easier. ANNE KARPF observes a new set of stereotypes.

UNTIL recently the world – or this corner of it – was an indisputably ageist place. The old were either benign grandparents or burdensome Alzheimer sufferers. Orthopaedic boots, walking-frames and Horlicks were their proper domain. But then it all began to change. The image of ageing became rejuvenated. Post-menopausal you might be, but post-aerobics? Never. Increasingly, old people are depicted not as dentured cronies but as leotarded achievers. But ageism hasn't gone away; it's had a face-lift.

If old people are now less likely to be invariably portrayed as passive victims, the new stereotype has stepped in smartly to take its place. Now the increasingly popular visual images of the old are on safari or climbing mountains; they effortlessly lap Olympic-sized pools, run marathons, complete Open University degrees, master Swahili.

At first, the new images seemed refreshing and liberating. It was a relief to know that you didn't have to swap denim for crimplene when the free bus pass arrived. The threshold of "old" visibly shifted, and the early images of the later Joan Collins and Jane Fonda seemed to totally redefine the lifespan: at the age when our foremothers were spent and sagging, these women were lithe and sizzling, effervescing with sex. But something wasn't right. The new way of valuing older people was to highlight their youthfulness. These older people were being celebrated for looking and acting young. Ageing had become a social crime.

In some ways this new stereotype of the "young old" is even more oppressive than the "old old" one was. Celebrities with their Hormone Replacement Therapy smiles and marathon-running pensioners may inspire some, but to others they represent an unattainable aspiration. And like the previous stereotypes, the new ones still lump old people together as a category rather than acknowledging their differences.

There's a seemingly charming story about the American feminist Gloria Steinem. On her 50th birthday an admirer came up and told her that she didn't look 50. "This is what 50 looks like," she retorted. I used to like that story until it struck me that she was wrong: no, this is what some 50-year-olds look like.

Those who've had materially or emotionally harder lives, who were widowed young or brought up kids alone, those whose genetic inheritance didn't include infinitely elastic skin or unshrinking bones, whose faces are mapped with past exertion and present fatigue, don't look like Gloria Steinem. But they shouldn't be punished for it.

The new images of ageing have brought their own ghastly truisms. Ladies and Gentlemen, You Are Only As Old As You Feel. They keep saying that. But what if you feel old?

If you feel old and have had enough, if life seems less inviting and more depleting, we'd rather not know. Just as we like our disabled people smiling and exceptional (the blind mountain-climber, the deaf musician) so we want the oldies that have bags of energy, who've never felt better, who are endlessly self-regenerating and "amazing for their age", not those who merely show it. (The revolution will have occurred when "you look your age" is a compliment.) We have reached such a pitch that instead of admiring and learning from those who feel they've had enough and are ready to die, we're forever trying to jolly them up and yank them back to life.

Look how they could be:

like the American 92-year-old featured last week on ITV's "First Tuesday" who's had 60 years of good health because, the doctors say, he's psychologically healthy. In the 1980s we were told it was our fault if we fell ill (we didn't eat properly or exercise enough); now it's our fault if we age. We lack the right attitudes or face cream.

But perhaps we shouldn't be hard on the new stereotype of ageing – it's only a response to the previous one. When everyone was portraying old people in a negative way, one antidote was to reverse the image, deny ageing, and remake the old as glamorous and athletic, even if for most old people in our society ageing is less about running a marathon and more about staff in residential homes intruding without knocking when residents are in the loo.

It's no return to the crimplene and Dundee cake image of old age that I'm touting. Clearly we are capable of living far more fully in old age than previous stereotypes allowed. Nor do I deny the importance of helping old people to retain their vitality and develop their creativity as long as they want. And, of course, there are the healthy old; I hope I'll be one of them. It's the preoccupation with the exceptional, those who defy their age, and our obsession with juvenescence that wants discarding. Peter Pan is not an appropriate icon for our greying times.

4

Choose the sentence which best expresses the main ideas of the passage.

The writer thinks that . . . :
1 . . . people should be allowed to grow old gracefully, preferably in good health, but should not feel that they have to look and feel young or glamorous.
2 . . . old people today are treated as if they are physically disabled or mentally ill when in fact they are perfectly healthy.
3 . . . old people should be encouraged to try to look and feel younger than they really are.

5

The words and expressions below are used to describe what the writer calls the *old old* and the *young old*. You may not understand some of them so you may need to use a dictionary, but they are all meant to create a positive or a negative image which you can guess from the context of the passage. Put a + sign or a − sign by each one according to the image it is meant to create.

1 benign grandparents
2 burdensome Alzheimer sufferers
3 dentured cronies
4 leotarded achievers
5 spent and sagging
6 lithe and sizzling, effervescing with sex

You can use a dictionary to check.

6

Decide which of these statements the author would agree with.

a) In western society old people used to be portrayed in a negative way.
b) The new youthful image of the elderly is liberating.
c) It is wrong for old people to want to look young.
d) The elderly are only as old as they feel.
e) Old people cannot all be considered in the same way.
f) Ageing is only a matter of a negative attitude.

Which ones do you agree with?

7

What do you think about the modern stereotype described in the passage? Would you say the writer is exaggerating?

What is the predominant image of old people in your country? Is it different from that described above? Is it more realistic?

What do you know about attitudes to old people in other parts of the world?

12 | My favourite place

1   In this unit, two writers, Germaine Greer and Jonathan Raban, write about their favourite places, Venice and Seattle.

   Here are some words and phrases which the writers use in their descriptions of the two places. Decide which ones come from the passage on Venice.

   salt-damp stone   gruff   crass   crest   hammered-gold sweep
   melancholy   indigo shadows   ornate   opalescent   foggy
   sleepy scent   law-abiding   sharp tang   crumbling stucco
   gloat   dazzle   timber suburbs

2   Imagine you're in Venice. What colours, sounds and smells come to mind? Now read the passage and find out if you chose the right words and phrases in Exercise 1.

3   Much of the description concentrates on the sights and atmosphere of Venice. For example, she writes:

   ... in winter you can feel the authentic Venetian melancholy ...
   ... and watch indigo shadows deepening on the Piazza San Marco ...

   She also focuses on the other senses. Write down the words and phrases she uses to talk about:

   sounds   tastes   smells

4   The writer creates a number of striking images to describe her favourite city. For example:

   ... the Venice of winter, when heels ring on salt-damp stone pavements that are colder than frozen.

   Which do you think is the strongest image?

VENICE

Venice is probably the most obvious of my favourite places, but my Venice is the Venice of winter, when heels ring on salt-damp stone pavements that are colder than frozen. Summer Venice is loud and crass; in winter you can feel the authentic Venetian melancholy, as sweet as it is bitter. Winter is the time to sit in the Café Florian over piping hot unsweetened chocolate hiding under a small alp of sugared *Schlag* and watch indigo shadows deepening on the Piazza San Marco, as the cadets from the police academy swing the dark blue capes of their Napoleonic dress uniform and chink their spurs, watching the women from under their cockaded tricornes.

In the morning you can run down to the *pescheria* and join the women scanning the opalescent heaps of glimmering fish and exotic crustaceans. The vendors will woo you to buy – "*Sposa! Bionda!*" – until they get what they seem to want really, a smile. As you go back to the Rialto you can sniff the sleepy scent of oranges and the sharp tang of winter salads brought down from the hills with the dew still on them. After that there are hundreds of places to go and spoils of mercantile empire to gloat over; if I can, I poke about in the Biblioteca Marciana, which is not to everybody's taste.

After lunch you can sit on the Zattere, shut your eyes against the dazzle of the low sun reflected off the Nile-green water and let it take the grey bloom off your winter skin. When you walk back to San Marco you will pass the flower stall at the bottom of the Accademia bridge, crammed to bursting with red roses, gardenia and tuberoses and you will realise with a pang like forgotten love that the street lamps of dying Venice are the faintest shade of rose.

Germaine Greer

5   Jonathan Raban, writing about his favourite place, Seattle, includes much
more factual information than Germaine Greer does about Venice.

Read the passage and note down any facts about Seattle. Which words or
phrases does the writer use to evoke the atmosphere?

6   Write down the one particular feature of Seattle which the writer likes.
Which of the senses does he use to describe the city?

7   Think of your favourite place and write a passage describing five of its
features focusing *not* on its sights, but on its sounds, tastes and smells. How
much do these senses contribute to your enjoyment of the place?

SEATTLE

Seattle is gruff in manners, Liberal Democratic in politics and piercingly beautiful in aspect. Built on a range of drowned mountain tops, it has boats at the end of its streets and the finest suburban rainbows in the world. As you crest a hill in Seattle (and you are always cresting hills in Seattle), you will be unfailingly surprised – by a turn-of-the-century version of the Uffizi or the Pitti Palace, by the hammered gold sweep of Puget Sound, by a white regatta on Lake Union. I am a water addict, and Seattle has more water, fresh and salt, than any place I know. Here, traffic stops to let ships and yachts go through splendid ornate lift-bridges; Indians lay salmon nets in the canal; my own boat is berthed a five-minute walk away from the house near the centre of town. There are more chandleries than boutiques, and on foggy winter days the commuter ferries turn into a mournful orchestra of warning diaphones.

It is a bookish city, with better bookstores than any in London or New York. The public library enforces a limit on borrowings – no more than a hundred to be taken out at any one time. It is also a deeply private city. People live here as if they were still in log cabins in the woods – in frame houses, hidden behind reserve that comes as a tonic after the bright gushiness of New York.

It is, on the whole, a law-abiding place – one of the very few American cities where you can safely walk the streets after dark. It goes in for serial murders rather than muggings; the typical Seattle criminal is the lonely psychopath, going about his nightly business with a logger's axe.

It is exactly as big now as Dickens's London was in the 1820s, and, like Dickens's London, it is a city of queer coincidences. I hope to set a novel in an imaginary city that will smell strongly of Seattle – a novel with water in it, and books, and murder, and crumbling stucco architecture, and spectacular fires in the timber suburbs, and angry hummingbirds at the feeder outside the window. For me, Seattle is the city I have always dreamed of. Where London is now unknowably big, Seattle is large and complex enough to be full of secrets, yet still sufficiently small to be encompassed in the imagination. It is one of the few cities left in the world that one might reasonably love.

Jonathan Raban

13 | Home town

1 In this unit there are some extracts from *The Lost Continent* by the contemporary writer, Bill Bryson, in which he describes his home town, Des Moines, and his home state, Iowa, as well as the characteristics of the people who live there.

First of all, think about your home town or region. Do you feel positive or negative about it? Make a list of its positive and negative points.

2 Read the first extract and decide if the writer's opinion of Des Moines is positive or negative.

> I come from Des Moines. Someone had to. When you come from Des Moines you either accept the fact without question and settle down with a local girl named Bobbi and get a job at the Firestone factory and live there forever and ever, or you spend your adolescence moaning at length about what a dump it is and how you can't wait to get out, and then you settle down with a local girl named Bobbi and get a job at the Firestone factory and live there forever and ever.
>
> Hardly anyone leaves. This is because Des Moines is the most powerful hypnotic known to man. Outside town there is a big sign that says: WELCOME TO DES MOINES. THIS IS WHAT DEATH IS LIKE. There isn't really. I just made that up. But the place does get a grip on you. People who have nothing to do with Des Moines drive in off the interstate, looking for gas or hamburgers, and stay forever. There's a New Jersey couple up the street from my parents' house whom you see wandering around from time to time looking faintly puzzled but strangely serene. Everybody in Des Moines is strangely serene.

3 Which of the following statements accurately describes the writer's opinion of Des Moines? (You can choose more than one.)

a) He is fatalistic about the lives of people who come from the town.
b) He finds the place unexciting.
c) People deliberately move to Des Moines because of the hamburgers and gas.
d) Des Moines attracts people from all over the USA.

4

Read the next extract and find out how the writer finds Des Moines in comparison with the rest of Iowa.

> When I was growing up I used to think that the best thing about coming from Des Moines was that it meant you didn't come from anywhere else in Iowa. By Iowa standards, Des Moines is a Mecca of cosmopolitanism, a dynamic hub of wealth and education, where people wear three-piece suits and dark socks, often simultaneously. During the annual state high school basketball tournament, when the hayseeds from out in the state would flood into the city for a week, we used to accost them downtown and snidely offer to show them how to ride an escalator or negotiate a revolving door. This wasn't so far from reality. My friend Stan, when he was about sixteen, had to go and stay with his cousin in some remote, dusty hamlet called Dog Water or Dunceville or some such improbable spot – the kind of place where if a dog gets run over by a truck everybody goes out to have a look at it. By the second week, delirious with boredom, Stan insisted that he and his cousin drive the fifty miles into the county town, Hooterville, and find something to do. They went bowling at an alley with warped lanes and chipped balls and afterwards had a chocolate soda and looked at a *Playboy* in a drugstore, and on the way home the cousin sighed with immense satisfaction and said, 'Gee thanks, Stan. That was the best time I ever had in my whole life.' It's true.

5

There may be some words you don't understand. Here are some questions to help you.

hub: In the context, it's another word for a place. To which place does it refer? Can you think of a simpler word?

hayseed: Here the word refers to people. Where do these people come from? Is the term likely to be a positive or a negative one?

accost: The verb suggests they established some contact with the *hayseeds*. Is it likely to be a friendly, impersonal or an aggressive contact?

snidely: Is the action likely to be done in a pleasant or a sarcastic way?

Dog Water, Dunceville, Hooterville: These are all fictitious places. Do they sound like places the writer recommends you to visit? Can you explain why or why not?

delirious: You use this word to describe someone who is ill with a high temperature and is talking nonsense. You can also talk about someone who is deliriously happy. What is its effect here?

warped, chipped: One expectation of a bowling alley is that it is straight and level, and of a bowling ball that it is round and smooth. So what are a bowling alley and ball likely to be in Hooterville? What else can you use these words to describe?

6 Read the next extract and write down words and phrases to describe the positive and negative aspects of the average Iowan's character.

I am not for a moment suggesting that Iowans are mentally deficient. They are a decidedly intelligent and sensible people who, despite their natural conservatism, have always been prepared to elect a conscientious, clear-thinking liberal in preference to some cretinous conservative. (...) And Iowans, I am proud to tell you, have the highest literacy rate in the nation: 99.5 per cent of grown-ups there can read. When I say they are kind of dopey, I mean that they are trusting and amiable and open. They are a tad slow, certainly – when you tell an Iowan a joke, you can see a kind of race going on between his brain and his expression – but it's not because they're incapable of high-speed mental activity, it's only that there isn't much call for it. Their wits are dulled by simple, wholesome faith in God and the soil and their fellow man.

Above all, Iowans are friendly. You go into a strange diner in the south and everything goes quiet, and you realize all the other customers are looking at you as if they are sizing up the risk involved in murdering you for your wallet and leaving your body in a shallow grave somewhere out in the swamps. In Iowa you are the centre of attention, the most interesting thing to hit town since a tornado carried off old Frank Sprinkel and his tractor last May. Everybody you meet acts like he would gladly give you his last beer and let you sleep with his sister. Everyone is strangely serene.

7 Underline the exaggerated comments in the extract above. Which do you find the most amusing?

8

Throughout the article the writer has described Des Moines in a very exaggerated way. Read the end of the article and find out how he really feels about the place.

On another continent, 4,000 miles away, I am quietly seized with that nostalgia that overcomes you when you have reached the middle of your life and your father has recently died and it dawns on you that when he went he took a part of you with him. I want to go back to the magic places of my youth – to Mackinac Island, Estes Park, Gettysburg – and see if they are as good as I remember them. I want to hear the long, low sound of a Rock Island locomotive calling across a still night, and the clack of it receding into the distance. I want to see lightning bugs, and hear cicadas shrilling, and be inescapably immersed in that hot, crazy-making August weather that makes your underwear scoot up every crack and fissure and cling to you like latex, and drives mild-mannered men to pull out hand guns in bars and light up the night with gunfire. I want to look for Ne-Hi Pop and Burma Shave signs and go to a ball game and sit at a marble-topped soda fountain and drive through the kind of small town that Deanna Durbin and Mickey Rooney used to live in in the movies. It's time to go home.

9

Look at the extracts again and write down any unexaggerated, more objective information that you can infer about the people and the place.

10

Think of a town in your country with features similar to those you wrote in Exercise 9. Make a list of all its features.

Now imagine that you have to attract visitors to the town. Write a short tourist brochure drawing people's attention to the town's appeal. Try and make even the negative features sound attractive.

14 | Looking for a rain god

1 The passage in this unit is a short story by Bessie Head, a South African writer who lived in Botswana until she died in 1986. The story, called *Looking For A Rain God*, was based on a local newspaper report.

Before you read the story, think about the title and look at these opening sentences from the first two paragraphs. What do you think the story is likely to be about?

> It is lonely at the lands where the people go
> to plough.
> The rains were late that year.

2 The following words appear in the story. Before you read it, decide whether they have positive, negative or neutral connotations. What do you think they may refer to?

shallow   shady   lush   tangled   dismal   powdery
anguish   scanty

3 **Read the first part of the story and see what the words actually refer to.**

It is lonely at the lands where the people go to plough. These lands are vast clearings in the bush, and the wild bush is lonely too. Nearly all the lands are within walking distance from the village. In some parts of the bush where the underground water is very near the surface, people made little rest camps for themselves and dug shallow wells to quench their thirst while on their journey to their own lands. They experienced all kinds of things once they left the village. They could rest at shady watering places full of lush, tangled trees with delicate pale-gold and purple wildflowers springing up between soft green moss and the children could hunt around for wild figs and any berries that might be in season. But from 1958, a seven-year drought fell upon the land and even the watering places began to look as dismal as the dry open thornbush country; the leaves of the trees curled up and withered; the moss became dry and hard and, under the shade of the tangled trees, the ground turned a powdery black and white because there was no rain. People said rather humorously that if you tried to catch the rain in a cup it would only fill a teaspoon. Toward the beginning of the seventh year of drought,

the summer had become an anguish to live through. The air was so dry and moisture-free that it burned the skin. No one knew what to do to escape the heat, and tragedy was in the air. At the beginning of that summer, a number of men just went out of their homes and hung themselves to death from trees. The majority of the people had lived off crops, but for two years past they had all returned from the lands with only their rolled-up skin blankets and cooking utensils. Only the charlatans, incanters and witch doctors made a pile of money during this time because people were always turning to them in desperation for little talismans and herbs to rub on the plough for the crops to grow and the rain to fall.

The rains were late that year. They came in early November, with a promise of good rain. It wasn't the full, steady downpour of the years of good rain but thin, scanty, misty rain. It softened the earth and a rich growth of green things sprang up everywhere for the animals to eat. People were called to the center of the village to hear the proclamation of the beginning of the ploughing season; they stirred themselves and whole families began to move off to the lands to plough.

4 **The story opens with a description of life in the bush before the drought years. What is the effect of this description?**

5 **Read the next part and look at the language the writer uses to describe how the rain ceased and the sun shone. What is striking about the description? What effect does it have?**

The family of the old man, Mokgobja, were among those who left early for the lands. They had a donkey cart and piled everything on to it: Mokgobja – who was over seventy years old; two girls, Neo and Boseyong; their mother Tiro and an unmarried sister, Nesta; and the father and supporter of the family, Ramadi, who drove the donkey cart. In the rush of the first hope of rain, the man, Ramadi, and the two women, cleared the land of thornbush and then hedged their vast ploughing area with this same thornbush to protect the future crop from the goats they had brought along for milk. They cleared out and deepened the old well with its pool of muddy water and still in this light, misty rain, Ramadi inspanned two oxen and turned the earth over with a hand plough.

The land was ready and ploughed, waiting for the crops. At night, the earth was alive with insects singing and rustling about in search of food. But suddenly, by mid-November, the rain flew away; the rain clouds fled away and left the sky bare. The sun danced dizzily in the sky, with a strange cruelty. Each day the land was covered in a haze of mist as the sun sucked up the last drop of moisture out of the earth. The family sat down in despair, waiting and waiting. Their hopes had run so high; the goats had started producing milk, which they had eagerly poured on their porridge, now they ate plain porridge with no milk. It was impossible to plant the corn, maize, pumpkin and watermelon seeds in the dry earth. They sat the whole day in the shadow of the huts and even stopped thinking, for the rain had fled away. Only the children, Neo and Boseyong, were quite happy in their little-girl world. They carried on with their game of making house like their mother and chattered to each other in light, soft tones. They made children from sticks around which they tied rags, and scolded them severely in an exact imitation of their own mother. Their voices could be heard scolding the day long: 'You stupid thing, when I send you to draw water, why do you spill half of it out of the bucket!' 'You stupid

thing! Can't you mind the porridge pot without letting the porridge burn!' And then they would beat the rag dolls on their bottoms with severe expressions.

The adults paid no attention to this; they did not even hear the funny chatter; they sat waiting for rain; their nerves were stretched to breaking point willing the rain to fall out of the sky. Nothing was important, beyond that. All their animals had been sold during the bad years to purchase food, and of all their herd only two goats were left. It was the women of the family who finally broke down under the strain of waiting for rain. It was really the two women who caused the death of the little girls. Each night they started a weird, high-pitched wailing that began on a low, mournful note and whipped up to a frenzy. Then they would stamp their feet and shout as though they had lost their heads. The men sat quiet and self-controlled; it was important for men to maintain their self-control at all times but their nerve was breaking too. They knew the women were haunted by the starvation of the coming year.

Finally, an ancient memory stirred in the old man, Mokgobja. When he was very young and the customs of the ancestors still ruled the land, he had been witness to a rainmaking ceremony. And he came alive a little, struggling to recall the details which had been buried by years and years of prayer in a Christian church. As soon as the mists cleared a little, he began consulting in whispers with his youngest son, Ramadi. There was, he said, a certain rain god who accepted only the sacrifice of the bodies of children. Then the rain would fall; then the crops would grow, he said. He explained the ritual and as he talked, his memory became a conviction and he began to talk with unshakeable authority. Ramadi's nerves were smashed by the nightly wailing of the women and soon the two men began whispering with the two women. The children continued their game: 'You stupid thing! How could you have lost the money on the way to the shop! You must have been playing again!'

6 The writer describes the changing mental state of the adults of the family from the *high hopes* at the beginning to despair then mental breakdown and finally renewed hope. Pick out the sentences which trace these changes. How do the reactions of the men differ from those of the women? What is striking about the way the children behave?

7 Read the last part of the story. How do the little girls die? Why does the writer say *It was really the two women who caused the death of the little girls*?

After it was all over and the bodies of the two little girls had been spread across the land, the rain did not fall. Instead, there was a deathly silence at night and the devouring heat of the sun by day. A terror, extreme and deep, overwhelmed the whole family. They packed, rolling up their skin blankets and pots, and fled back to the village.

People in the village soon noted the absence of the two little girls. They had died at the lands and were buried there, the family said. But people noted their ashen, terror-stricken faces and a murmur arose. What had killed the children, they wanted to know? And the family replied that they had just died. And people said amongst themselves that it was strange that the two deaths had occurred at the same time. And there was a feeling of great unease at the unnatural looks of the family. Soon the police came around. The family told them the same story of death and burial at the lands. They did not know what the children had died of. So the police asked to see the graves. At this, the mother of the children broke down and told everything.

Throughout that terrible summer the story of the children hung like a dark cloud of sorrow over the village, and the sorrow was not assuaged when the old man and Ramadi were sentenced to death for ritual murder. All they had on the statute books was that ritual murder was against the law and must be stamped out with the death penalty. The subtle story of strain and starvation and breakdown was inadmissible evidence at court; but all the people who lived off crops knew in their hearts that only a hair's breadth had saved them from sharing a fate similar to that of the Mokgobja family. They could have killed something to make the rain fall.

8 How has the mental state of the family changed? What is more important to them now – their crops or their crime?

How does the writer relate the death of the little girls? Is the tone matter-of-fact or is it emotionally charged?

9 Look at the statements below. Which do you think best defines the theme the writer develops in the story?

- A dreadful crime in the African bush
- The psychological extremes of human endurance
- Superstition in rural Africa
- Drought in Africa

10 The story was based on a report in a local newspaper. Look back at the story and decide what information appeared in the original article. What has the writer added? Write the story in the form of a newspaper article.

15 | Mirror

1 The poems in this unit are by Sylvia Plath, the American poet (1932–63) and
Robert Graves, the English writer and poet (1895–1985). The titles of the
poems are *Mirror* and *The Face in the Mirror*. What do you think they're
about? Write down six words you would use in a poem with a similar title.

2 *Mirror* is written in the first person. Read the poem and decide who *I* refers
to.

Mirror

I am silver and exact. I have no preconceptions.
Whatever I see I swallow immediately
Just as it is, unmisted by love or dislike.
I am not cruel; only truthful –
The eye of a little god, four-cornered.
Most of the time I meditate on the opposite wall.
It is pink, with speckles. I have looked at it so long
I think it is a part of my heart. But it flickers.
Faces and darkness separate us over and over.

Now I am a lake. A woman bends over me,
Searching my reaches for what she really is.
Then she turns to those liars, the candles or the moon.
I see her back and reflect it faithfully.
She rewards me with tears and an agitation of hands.
I am important to her. She comes and goes.
Each morning it is her face that replaces the darkness.
In me she has drowned a young girl, and in me an old woman
Rises towards her day after day like a terrible fish.

Sylvia Plath

3 Answer the following questions.

1 Read stanza 1 again and write down six words or expressions which convey the impression that the mirror is a person. What effect does this device have?

2 What is: 'unmisted by love or dislike'?
            'four-cornered'?
            'pink, with speckles'?

3 Why is the mirror likened to 'The eye of a little god'?

4 What is the mirror likened to in the second stanza? Find words which build up this image.

5 Why are the candles and the moon referred to as 'liars'?
Why does the woman reward the mirror with 'tears and an agitation of hands'?

4 What is the main idea of the poem? Does it deal with any other ideas?

5 Did you enjoy the poem? Can you explain why or why not?

6 Read *The Face in the Mirror* and decide who is speaking and what he or she is doing.

The Face in the Mirror

Grey haunted eyes, absent-mindedly glaring
From wide, uneven orbits; one brow drooping
Somewhat over the eye
Because of a missile fragment still inhering,
Skin deep, as a foolish record of old-world fighting.

Crookedly broken nose – low tackling caused it;
Cheeks, furrowed; course grey hair, flying frenetic;
Forehead, wrinkled and high;
Jowls, prominent; ears, large; jaws, pugilistic;
Teeth, few; lips, full and ruddy; mouth, ascetic.

I pause with razor poised, scowling derision
At the mirrored man whose beard needs my attention,
And once more ask him why
He still stands ready, with a boy's presumption,
To court the queen in her high silk pavilion.

Robert Graves

7 In stanzas 1 and 2 the speaker describes his own face. First, identify the particular features, then decide if the words and expressions he uses are unflattering, flattering or neutral. Put them in the right columns below. You can use a dictionary.

Unflattering	Flattering	Neutral
uneven		wide

Is the overall description flattering or unflattering?

8 In stanza 3 the speaker comments on his own reflection. What is his attitude? Why does it explain the type of description he gave of himself in the first two stanzas?

He uses the third person 'he' to refer to his reflection. What effect does this have?

9 What is the common theme of both poems? Which poem do you like best?

10 What words or phrases would you use to describe your own face in a flattering, unflattering and neutral way?

11 The next poem, by Thomas Hardy, the English poet and novelist (1840–1928), is on the same theme. Read it for your pleasure. You can use a dictionary to help you.

I Look into my Glass

I look into my glass,
And view my wasting skin,
And say, 'Would God it come to pass
My heart had shrunk as thin!'

For then, I, undistrest
By hearts grown cold to me,
Could lonely wait my endless rest
With equanimity.

But Time, to make me grieve,
Part steals, lets part abide;
And shakes this fragile frame at eve
With throbbings of noontide.

Thomas Hardy

16 | Colours

1   How important is colour to you? Think about your answers to these questions.

— Is there a predominant colour in your home or in your choice of clothes?
— Have you changed your favourite colours in recent years?
— Do you buy clothes in 'fashionable' colours?
— Do you prefer bright or pastel colours?
— Do you like mixing different colours or different tones?
— What are the fashionable colours in your country this year? Are you wearing any of them?

2   Read the passage by Roger Tredre and decide which of these statements are true.

1   Climate and skin colour are important for determining colour preferences.
2   Colour predictions for the fashion market are now made on a European scale.
3   National specificity is maintained by mixing the colours differently.
4   Daniel Hechter is very much appreciated in Britain.
5   National colour sense changes little over the years.
6   Pink has only been associated with femininity since the Thirties.
7   Pastel colours always sell well.
8   The experts predict European colour fashion from one year to the next.
9   The British bad colour sense is improving.

By their colours you shall know them

1   COLOURS divide Europeans, just as surely as languages. The confident Germans like theirs bright and sharp: ruby red, vermilion, pine green. The sophisticated Italians like olive green, pumpkin, ecru. The cautious British feel at home with navy blue and brown.

2   Never mind 1992: a Europe *sans frontières* colourwise remains a distant prospect. Fashion companies that sell in more than one country need to be alert to different national tastes in colour.

What causes a colour to be more popular in one country? "Climate and skin colour," says Philippa Watkins, a senior lecturer in textiles at the Royal College of Art in London: "The long Italian summers, and olive skins of the people are perfectly suited to deep, rich colours or very bright colours." However, colour forecasters are speculating that if the greenhouse effect produces lasting climatic change, national colour preferences could radically reorientate. 3

4   The recent succession of sunny summers in Britain has already prompted sales of very bright colours, once considered unsuitable for our grey skies.

There are more deep-rooted forces at work, too, linked to each nation's history, geography and religion. Why do the Greeks love blue? Blue is the colour of the Greek flag and Greek Orthodoxy. But it is also the colour of the Greek sky most of the year, and the famously beautiful Aegean.

The expert colour forecasters try to bear in mind national colour preferences. "By their very nature, European-wide colour predictions are something of a compromise," says Stephen Higginson, who coordinates the International Colour Authority's biannual publication. "Each country will emphasise different parts of the palette we produce."

Often, it's the mix of colours that makes all the difference. A young French yuppie *(bon chic, bon genre)* mixes greens and purples in a manner that seems quite startling to British eyes. I am convinced that Daniel Hechter's use of green explains why the well-known French designer has never made much headway on this side of the Channel.

The problem is that just as soon as ground rules about a nation's sense of colour have been drawn up, they have to be rewritten. Peter Lefevre, a leading authority on colour with the International Wool Secretariat in Paris, points out that the French once believed that it was bad luck to wear green.

Colour is changing colour before our eyes. Think pink, and think again. Pink came of age in the Thirties under the tutelage of Elsa Schiaparelli. With the invention of "shocking pink", the Italian fashion designer did away with the colour's longtime association with sweet, docile femininity. Her pink "shocked" because it was of an unimagined vibrancy: a hot, bold colour for a brash new age.

Half a century on, pink is different. Schiaparelli's brand of pink no longer "shocks". That pink that so amazed in the Thirties seems tame indeed alongside the sizzling shades now on offer. After living through the colours of the psychedelic Sixties, and more than one revival of eye-dazzling neons and day-glo brights, we are all turning into colour trippers. Colour television and coloured graphics have accustomed our eyes to new intensities of colour barely imaginable in the Thirties.

Many of the new fashion colours – the ones we will be wearing next spring – were bright beyond belief in Florence this month at Pitti Immagine Filati, the yarn trade exhibition. Here fashion manufacturers were playing their seasonal game of trying to predict the market, and the colour specialists had run out of superlatives for such a profusion of vibrant reds, yellows and purples. *International Textiles,* the trade monthly, found the best description: "felt-tip colours".

Pre-guessing colours is a tricky, inexact business. Colour sells clothes, but no one knows for sure what will sell, and when. The unwary retailer who puts a range of pastel cardigans into the shops in April might make heavy losses if it rains throughout the month.

Forecasters have to take into account a broad diversity of themes, which may influence the customer's choice. These range from intangibles – something in the air, the international *zeitgeist* – to specifics such as important designers' collections, exhibitions or popular films ("Out of Africa" prompted a surge in demand for the colours of the savannah).

The key colours for fashion and interiors are determined by a handful of colour experts, who spend their time travelling the world picking up inspiration and trying to spot trends. They meet twice a year to predict the colours the Europeans will all want to wear, or be surrounded by, two years hence. Their ideas are, in turn, picked up and developed by yarn manufacturers.

It is often suggested that we British have an underdeveloped sense of colour. A stroll down any town high street on a Saturday morning can be depressing: there is every colour of the rainbow, garishly mixed in a manner calculated to offend the sensibilities of the purist. But the picture is more encouraging than it seems. Recent years have seen a quiet revolution in our sense of colour, marked by a greater willingness on the part of retailers such as Marks and Spencer, BHS and Habitat to explore and experiment.

Julie Buddy, a leading American colour specialist who has been living in Europe since the Sixties, remembers when British retailers were more stubborn. In 1976, she tried to persuade Debenhams to put yellow in a spring fashion range. "They threw me out of the door."

In 1980, Littlewoods was equally sceptical about Ms Buddy's suggestions for a range of peach-coloured knitwear. But it sold well. "We did sweaters in peach, baby turquoise blue and soft buttercup yellow," she recalls, describing the tones with the ease that comes naturally to colour professionals.

Designers, both in fashion and interiors, are now working with colour with more sophistication. Craig Leeson, a young Englishman who designs for Reporter, one of Italy's most successful menswear labels, says: "Once upon a time, there was red and green and yellow. Now designers are exploring *tones* rather than the obvious primary colours."

Mr Leeson is now playing with blue, a very popular colour for this summer. "The base colour is blue, but it's blue with 20 different tones; more like aquamarine, eggshell blue, petrol blue, denim blue."

This new sophistication may, perhaps, hold the key for the future of colour. Hand in hand with the development of ever-brighter colours, the next decade will see a movement towards greater sophistication and subtlety in fashion colours. After all, can pink get that much pinker?

3 Read the passage again and find out what colours people from Germany, Italy, Britain and Greece like and the possible reasons.

If you come from one of these countries, do you agree? If you come from another country, do you think there is a national preference for a particular colour?

4 There are a number of words or expressions in this passage which you may not be familiar with. Use the clues below to help you guess the general meaning of some of them.

1 *startling* (paragraph 7): What is startling? Do the British find this familiar or surprising?
2 *brash* (paragraph 9): Which adjectives in the same sentence have a similar meaning in the context of the passage?
3 *tame* (paragraph 10): What were colours like in the Thirties? Are they likely to have been more or less exciting than colours today?
4 *colour-trippers* (paragraph 10): In this context, a tripper is a word more frequently used when referring to someone who has taken drugs. How has our contact with colour changed in recent years? Does the use of the word suggest that we are exposed to few or lots of colours?
5 *run out of superlatives* (paragraph 11): The colours were all extremely bright. What sort of words were the specialists likely to use when describing these colours?
6 *felt-tip* (paragraph 11): This refers to a type of coloured pen. In the context of the paragraph are felt-tip colours likely to be strong or pastel?
7 *surge* (paragraph 13): Is this likely to be a strong increase or decrease in demand?
8 *garishly* (paragraph 15): Is this likely to be tasteful or not?
9 *stubborn* (paragraph 16): Were the British stores willing to sell new colours?

You can use your dictionary to check.

5

Put the sentences below in the correct order to make a summary of the passage.

a) The great variety of colours now available for interiors and fashion clothes means that there is less scope for innovation with the primary colours.

b) These are then adapted to suit the tastes of the individual countries.

c) The experts are now looking more closely at mixing different tones for future designs.

d) Colour tastes vary from one European country to another.

e) People have gradually become accustomed to colours which were previously considered unacceptable.

f) A number of factors appear to determine these national preferences including the climate and skin colour. Even a nation's history, geography or religion may have an influence.

g) Because of these variations the fashion designers can only predict general trends at a European level.

h) By experimenting with different colours and tones, the designers have greatly influenced colour sense in recent years.

i) However, many of these unwritten rules are continually changing before our eyes.

6

Colours have different meanings in different cultures. For example, white is the colour of death in parts of Africa; in the West it is black. A black cat is lucky in Britain, in the USA it is unlucky; red is a lucky colour in China.

What colours do you associate with the following?

good luck   danger   cowardice   innocence   cold   heat
passion   naivety   your country

17 | The new world

1 The story in this unit is by Alasdair Gray, a contemporary Scottish writer. Look at the title and the first two sentences.

> ### The New World
>
> MILLIONS of people lived in rooms joined by windowless corridors. The work which kept their world going (or seemed to, because they were taught that it did, and nobody can teach the exact truth) was done on machines in the rooms where they lived, and the machines rewarded them by telling them how much they earned.

What do you expect the story to be about? Do you expect it to be optimistic or pessimistic?

2 Read on and think about where it is set.

> Big earners could borrow money which got them better rooms. The machines, the moneylending and most of the rooms belonged to three or four organisations. There was also a government and a method of choosing it which allowed everyone, every five years, to press a button marked STAY or CHANGE. This kept or altered the faces of their politicians. The politicians paid themselves for governing, and also drew incomes from the organisations which owned everything, but governing and owning were regarded as separate activities, so the personal links between them were dismissed as coincidences or accepted as inevitable. Yet many folk – even big earners in comfortable rooms – felt enclosed without knowing exactly what enclosed them. When the government announced that it now governed a wholly new world many people were greatly excited, because their history associated new worlds with freedom and wide spaces.

3

Which of the following words would you use to describe the political, social and economic structure of the society in which the story is set?

democratic   communist   socialist   fascist   capitalist
bureaucratic   oppressive   enlightened   just   hard-working
hierarchical   Utopian

4

Where do you think this *wholly new world* might be?

5

Read the rest of the story and answer the questions.

I imagine a man, not young or especially talented, but intelligent and hopeful, who pays for the privilege of emigrating to the new world. This costs nearly all he has, but in the new world he can win back four times as much in a few years if he works extra hard. He goes to a room full of people like himself. Eventually a door slides open and they filter down a passage to the interior of their transport. It resembles a small cinema. The emigrés sit watching a screen on which appears deep blackness spotted with little lights, the universe they are told they are travelling through. One of the lights grows so big that it is recognisable as a blue and white cloud-swept globe whose surface is mainly un-reflecting ocean, then all lights are extinguished and, without alarm, our man falls asleep. He has been told that a spell of unconsciousness will ease his arrival in the new world.

1 Do you think they are really travelling or is it an illusion? Are they going to or leaving Earth?

He awakens on his feet, facing a clerk across a counter. The clerk hands him a numbered disc, points to a corridor, and tells him to walk down it and wait outside a door with the same number. These instructions are easy to follow. Our man is so stupefied by his recent sleep that he walks a long way before remembering he is supposed to be in a new world. It is perhaps a different world, for the corridor is narrower than the corridors he is used to, and coloured matt brown instead of shiny green, but it has the same lack of windows. The only new thing he notices is a strong smell of fresh paint.

2 Where do you think they are? Why is the paint fresh? Is it a trick?

He walks very far before finding the door. A man of his own sort sits on a bench in front of it staring morosely at the floor between his shoes. He does not look up when our man sits beside him. A long time passes. Our man grows impatient. The corridor is so narrow that his knees are not much more than a foot from the door he faces. There is nothing to look at but brown paintwork. At length he murmurs sarcastically,

"So this is our new world." His neighbour glances at him briefly with a quick shake of the head. An equally long time passes before our man says, almost explosively, "They promised me more room! Where is it? Where is it?" The door opens, an empty metal trolley is pushed obliquely through and smashes hard into our man's legs. With a scream he staggers to his feet and hobbles backwards away from the trolley, which is pushed by someone in a khaki dustcoat who is so big that his shoulders brush the walls on each side and also the ceiling; the low ceiling makes the trolley-pusher bend his head so far forward that our man, retreating sideways now and stammering words of pain and entreaty, stares up not at a face but at a bloated bald scalp. He cannot see if his pursuer is brutally herding him or merely pushing a trolley. In sheer panic our man is about to yell for help when a voice says, "What's happening here? Leave the man alone, Henry!" and his hand is seized in a comforting grip. The pain in his legs vanishes at once, or is forgotten.

His hand is held by another man of his own type, but a sympathetic and competent one who is leading him away from the trolleyman. Our man, not yet recovered from a brutal assault of the kind he has only experienced in childhood, is childishly grateful for the pressure of the friendly hand. "I'm sure you were doing nothing wrong," says the stranger. "You were probably just complaining. Henry gets cross when he hears one of our sort complain. Class prejudice is the root of it. What were you complaining about? Lack of space, perhaps?"

Our man looks into the friendly, guileless face beside him and, after a moment, nods: which may be the worst mistake of his life, but for a while he does not notice this.

The comforting hand clasp, the increasing distance from Henry who falls further behind with each brisk step they take, is accompanied by a feeling that the corridors are becoming spacious, the walls further apart, the ceiling higher. His companion also seems larger and for a while this too is a comfort, a return to the safety of childhood when he was protected by bigger people who liked him. But he is shrinking, and the smaller he gets the more desperately he clutches the hand which is reducing his human stature. At last, when the arm is dragged so straight above his head that in another moment it will swing him clear of the floor, his companion releases him, smiles down at him, wags a kindly forefinger and says, "Now you have all the space you need. But remember, God is trapped in you! He will not let you rest until you amount to more than this."

The stranger goes through a door, closing it carefully after him. Our man stares up at the knob on it which is now and forever out of his reach.

3 Who do you think these people are? What's going to happen next?

4 Why is this a mistake? What's going to happen?

6 Answer the questions.

1 In which sentence does he first realise that things are not quite what he expected?
2 Which is the sentence which confirms his suspicions?
3 Underline the adjectives which describe *our man*'s feelings about the man who leads him away by the hand.
4 Which clause suggests to the reader that the friendly man is not going to be so friendly after all?
5 Which sentence shows that *our man* realises this as well?
6 In one sense, *our man* achieves what he aspires to. How? In another sense, it seems he is being punished. What is his crime?

7

"Now you have all the space you need. But remember, God is trapped in you! He will not let you rest until you amount to more than this."

What does this mean? What comment is the writer making on society, life and human aspirations?

Did you find the story frightening, sad, incomprehensible?

8

Imagine this is not the end of the story. How do you think it might continue? Write a few sentences giving the story a different ending.

18 | Take my tip

1 **The passage in this unit, which is by the English writer Keith Waterhouse, appeared in *High Life* magazine. It is about tipping. Before you read the passage answer these questions about tipping in your country.**

- Who do you tip?
- How much do you give?
- How do you tip?
- Why do you tip?

How do you feel about the habit of tipping? Do you keep to the rules on tipping in your country? Which circumstances encourage or discourage you from tipping?

2 **The title is a play on words and has two meanings. Check you understand both meanings.**

3 **Look quickly through the passage and find out which paragraphs discuss the questions in Exercise 1.**

1 The first time I was ever taken out to a café, at the age of around four, I thought I had hit gold. There under the saucer was a whole threepenny bit – left for me, I surmised, by the tooth fairy.

2 My mother explained that it was a tip for the waitress from the table's previous occupant. When we rose to leave, she too placed a threepenny bit under the saucer, as surreptitiously as a secret agent leaving a cache of microfilm for a confederate. I was fascinated by the furtiveness of the transaction and grew up in the baffled belief that tipping was a mystique known only to its practitioners, like some black magic rite.

As indeed it is. While tipping is more overt these days – you leave your offering on a plate for all to see rather than tucking it under your saucer, and your waitress brazenly bears it off before

3 your very eyes instead of waiting until you have slunk off the premises – it is still a code, a ritual, an exercise in the monetary equivalent of body language.

4 The diner who, on settling his bill, adds 15% plus a bit to round the total up to the nearest fiver, is not merely leaving a tip. He is making a statement. He is saying, "See how generous I am," or "See how rich I am," or "I want to buy your esteem." Rarely is he simply saying in a straightforward way, "I enjoyed the meal."

The waiter who, on presenting the said bill, scrawls all over it in red letters, SERVICE NOT INCLUDED, is not merely demanding a tip. He is saying, "I have had it up to here with cheapskates who try to get out without tipping. What do they think this is – a free soup kitchen?" The same waiter, transferring his allegiance to an establish-

70

5 ment where a service charge is included, will leave the credit card voucher total open. He is saying, like Oliver Twist, "Please sir, I want more." Or, more subtly if even more shamelessly: "I've got you sussed out as someone who doesn't have the confidence to pay the going rate without adding a bit on for luck. Here's your opportunity to impress your girlfriend."

Forget any idea that tipping is first and foremost a reward for services rendered. It is self-

6 indulgence, it is showing-off, it is cowardice, it is expediency, it is surrender to extortion, it is social inadequacy. With service to be added at the customer's discretion.

I am by no means averse to tipping (as distinct from the obligatory service charge, which is very often not wholly distributed among staff, which in turn is why some waiters appear to be soliciting for alms when you think you have already recompensed them), and indeed prefer a tipping society to a non-tipping one. You may not know what you are doing in a tipping society but at least you

7 know where you are – that man in the peaked cap requires you to dip your hand in your pocket. But in a non-tipping environment such as Iceland or China you never know quite what they want of you. How can you be sure that Iceland is not gradually changing its approach to gratuities like Israel, where you now tip hotel functionaries when once you didn't! In New Zealand on a recent trip I found some barmen pushing my tip back across the counter, others pocketing it as if by right.

Where do we stand, that's what we want to know about tipping. In American bars, as distinct from British pubs, it is customary, nay, obligatory, to tip, and I have heard more than one neglectful departing drinker summoned back with a stentorian cry from the barman of *"Hey! Gratooity!"* (I was once present in a Miami bar when the reminder was uttered to a burly New Yorker who had just exchanged a package holi

8 day voucher for a free drink. His snarled response was, "So what's fifteen per cent of nuthin'?") The British system, where one invites the barman (or more likely the barmaid) to "have one yourself" only after an unusually complex round or after a certain rapport has been established, is a subtle and should I say more civilised one. But at least you know where you are with the American barman – and it is not knowing where you are that bedevils this whole business of tipping.

What we all need to know is who to tip and how much. It can be an embarrassing business but I do not think we need to waste any time sympathising with former US President Reagan who on a visit to China was pursued down the street by a shopkeeper determined to return his tip. No one needs to tip shopkeepers, whether in China or anywhere else. Tips, to my mind anyway, should be largely reserved for those performing a service who would otherwise be inadequately paid for it – waiters, doormen, cloakroom attendants and the like. The concept varies from country to country. In France you tip theatre

9 usherettes. In Egypt you tip the hotel commissionaire's brother for hanging around the place opening doors. In the United States you tip the restaurant *maitre d'* who probably earns more than you do. But the principle is there to be followed: a tip for those who have earned one and look as if they expect it (watch for subtle hints such as an extended palm or a doffed hat); no tip for those who have performed no personal service. (On my first ever trip abroad as a callow young man, staying on expenses in a very grand hotel, I tipped the lift attendant in my confusion. His amazed expression was a crash course on where the tipping has to stop.)

How much? The American dollar bill might have been invented for the purpose of tipping porters or bellboys, doormen hailing taxis, taxi drivers themselves on a shortish journey. It is the perfect tipping unit – convertible up or down into

10 most currencies of the world. In the UK, I am afraid, it is now convertible in an upward direction, with the pound coin rapidly becoming the common small-change tip rather than the 50p piece.

In restaurants, I have begun to resist the notion, which has filtered over from New York and Los Angeles, that 15% is "about right". Outside London 12½% or even 10% is still considered "about right" (though I always feel that 10% is neither one thing nor the other – you feel obliged

11 to bump it up a bit and finish up tipping 20% or so in all). But while 15% is acceptable on a meal for two on the right side of £50, it becomes a bit steep when the bill itself becomes steeper – especially since Value Added Tax is included every step of the way.

If a bill for £100 – not unusual these days – yields a service charge of £15, not only is it very likely exorbitant but it is also extortionate. The £100 bill includes 15% tax and so is only £86.95 nett. 15% of the overall bill is £15. You have over

12 tipped by £3. Maybe that was not the Government's intention when they insisted that VAT charges must be built into all restaurant bills; but if it was not your intention that they should be built into all tips also, carry a pocket calculator.

Or contrive to eat in-flight. Your cabin crew do

13 not expect gratuities!

Do people in other countries tip in the same way as you do?

4

Read the passage again and make notes on tipping habits in the following countries.

The United States   Britain   France   Egypt

5

Answer the questions.

1 What is the advantage of the American system?
2 What is the disadvantage of the British system?
3 How can you recognise someone who should receive a tip?

6

In each of these sentences from the passage there is a word or an expression missing. Without looking back at the article, try and find suitable words to fill the blanks.

1   ... and I have heard more than one neglectful departing drinker summoned back with a .... cry from the barman of *"Hey! Gratooity!"*

2   ... and it is not knowing where you are that .... this whole business of tipping.

3   On my first ever trip abroad as a .... young man, ... I tipped the lift attendant in my confusion.

4   ... I always feel that 10% is neither one thing nor the other – you feel obliged to .... it up a bit and finish up tipping 20% or so in all.

5   If a bill for £100 – not unusual these days – yields a service charge of £15, not only is it very likely exorbitant but it is also ....

Now look at the article again. Did you choose the same words? Do you understand the words in the passage? You can use your dictionary to check.

7

List the people who you tip but would prefer not to. Can you explain why not? Then think of people who you would like to tip, but perhaps don't, e.g. doctors, dentists, bus drivers, teachers. Give your reasons.

19 | Pilgrim at Tinker Creek

1 The passage in this unit comes from *Pilgrim at Tinker Creek*, by Annie Dillard, a contemporary American author who lived in the Roanoke Valley of Virginia, the area she describes below, when she wrote this. The passage describes in elaborate detail the sights and sounds of the woods and rivers as the light of a warm summer's day begins to fade.

Here are some words from the first part of the passage. What atmosphere do they create?

creek   shallow   bloom   fish   reptiles   windless
stillness

Imagine that you are standing quietly in a wood as the warm summer night falls. What can you see and hear?

2 Read the first part of the text and write a single sentence saying what the writer often does at Tinker Creek.

> Where Tinker Creek flows under the sycamore log bridge to the tear-shaped island, it is slow and shallow, fringed thinly in cattail marsh. At this spot an astonishing bloom of life supports vast breeding populations of insects, fish, reptiles, birds and mammals. On windless summer evenings I stalk along the creek bank or straddle the sycamore log in absolute stillness, watching for muskrat.

3 Here are some words from the next part which the writer uses to describe what she feels and what she sees.

spellbound   reflection   materialized   floating   smooth
gliding   weightless   streamers

How would you describe her mood? Do you expect her to be watching something in particular or simply taking in the atmosphere?

4 Read on and check your answers to Exercise 3.

> The night I stayed too late I was hunched on the log staring spellbound at spreading, reflected stains of lilac on the water. A cloud in the sky suddenly lighted as if turned on by a switch; its reflection just as suddenly materialized on the water upstream, flat and floating, so that I couldn't see the creek bottom, or the life in the water under the cloud. Downstream, away from the cloud on the water, water turtles smooth as beans were gliding down with the current in a series of easy, weightless push-offs, as men bound on the moon. I didn't know whether to trace the progress of one turtle I was sure of, risking sticking my face in one of the bridge's spider webs made invisible by the gathering dark, or take chance of seeing the carp, or scan the mudbank in hope of seeing a muskrat, or follow the last of the swallows who caught at my heart and trailed it after them like streamers as they appeared from directly below, under the log, flying upstream with their tails forked, so fast.

Write another single sentence saying what the writer was doing that evening.

5 This part begins:

The night I stayed too late ...

What do you expect to happen next?

Read the next part and find out if you were right.

> But shadows spread and deepened and stayed. After thousands of years we're still strangers to darkness, fearful aliens in an enemy camp with our arms crossed over our chests. I stirred. A land turtle on the bank, startled, hissed the air from its lungs and withdrew to its shell. An uneasy pink here, and unfathomable blue there, gave great suggestion of lurking beings. Things were going on. I couldn't see whether that rustle I heard was a distant rattlesnake, slit-eyed, or a nearby sparrow kicking in the dry flood debris slung at the foot of a willow. Tremendous action roiled the water everywhere I looked, big action, inexplicable. A tremor welled beside a gaping muskrat burrow in the bank and I caught my breath, but no muskrat appeared. The ripples continued to fan upstream with a steady, powerful thrust. Night was knitting an eyeless mask over my face, and I still sat transfixed. A distant airplane, a delta wing out of a nightmare, made a gliding shadow on the creek's bottom that looked like a stingray cruising upstream. At once a black fin slit the pink cloud on the water, shearing it in two. The two halves merged together and seemed to dissolve before my eyes. Darkness pooled in the cleft of the creek and rose, as water collects in a well. Untamed, dreaming lights flickered over the sky. I saw hints of hulking underwater shadows, two pale splashes out of the water, and round ripples rolling close together from a blackened center.

6 **Try to distinguish between what is actually happening and everything else the writer feels or sees. Write down the phrases or sentences which describe what's going on. The sequence of events starts with:**

'A land turtle on the bank . . . withdrew to its shell.' . . .

7 **Read the second and third parts of the passage again and note down all the animals and other wildlife mentioned.**

8 **What do you expect to happen next? Read on and find out.**

> At last I stared upstream where only the deepest violet remained of the cloud, a cloud so high its underbelly still glowed, its feeble color reflected from a hidden sky lighted in turn by a sun halfway to China. And out of that violet, a sudden enormous black body arced over the water. Head and tail, if there was a head and tail, were both submerged in cloud. I saw only one ebony fling, a headlong dive into darkness; then the waters closed, and the lights went out.

Write a single sentence describing what the writer saw.

9 Read the end of the passage and answer the questions.

> I walked home in a shivering daze, up hill and down. Later I lay open-mouthed in bed, my arms flung wide at my sides to steady the whirling darkness. At this latitude I'm spinning 836 miles an hour round the earth's axis; I feel my sweeping fall as a breakneck arc like the dive of dolphins, and the hollow rushing of wind raises the hairs on my neck and the side of my face. In orbit around the sun I'm moving 64,800 miles an hour. The solar system as a whole, like a merry-go-round unhinged, spins, bobs, and blinks at the speed of 43,200 miles an hour along a course set east of Hercules. Someone has piped, and we're dancing a tarantella until the sweat pours. I open my eyes and I see dark, muscled forms curl out of water, with flapping gills and flattened eyes. I close my eyes and I see stars, deep stars giving way to deeper stars, deeper stars bowing to deepest stars at the crown of an infinite cone.

1 '... I lay open-mouthed in bed, my arms flung wide at my sides ...'   What sense does this convey of how she feels about the incident earlier that evening?
2 What is the effect of suddenly introducing scientific facts about the speed of the earth's rotation, etc.?

10 How would you describe the writer's style? Do you like it?

11 Use the phrases and sentences you wrote in Exercises 2, 4, 6 and 8 to write a summary describing the setting and the main sequence of events, the 'bare bones' of what the writer describes.

20 | The new café

1 The story in this unit is by the novelist Doris Lessing. As this is the last unit in *Reading 4*, we hope you feel more confident about your reading skills. There are fewer exercises than usual, and the questions are designed simply to draw your attention to interesting features of the story.

Read the story for your own enjoyment.

The new café

THERE IS a new café in our main street, Stephanie's, a year old now, and always full. It is French, like the "Boucherie" next to it – a very British butcher – like the "Brasserie" opposite, and it is run by two Greeks. At once it acquired its regulars, of whom I am one. Here, as in all good cafés, may be observed real-life soap operas, to be defined as a series of emotional events that are certainly not unfamiliar, since you are bound to have seen something like them before, but to which you lack the key that will make them not trite, but shockingly individual.

Last summer, the miraculous summer of 1989, when one hot blue day followed another, made pavement life as intense as in Paris or Rome, and our café had tables outside, crammed against the aromatic offerings of a greengrocer. There everyone prefers to sit, but you are lucky to find a seat. Early in summer two German girls appeared, large, attractive, uninhibitedly in search of boyfriends for their holidays. They were always together, usually outside, and for a few days sat alone eating the delicious cakes – genuinely French – that none can resist. They were delighted when someone – anyone – said, "Is this chair free?" Once this was me. They had three weeks in London. They were in a small hotel ten minutes away. They thought London a fine place. The weather was wonderful and – look! – how brown we are getting. While they chatted their eyes at once flew to anyone coming.

And then they were with a young man. I had seen him here before. He sometimes dropped in for a coffee and was off at once. The German girls liked him. They leaned forward on their large and confident behinds and laughed and flung back blonde manes and their rows of dewy teeth shone out at everybody. For they continued to keep an eye on possibilities. He leaned back in his chair, legs hooked around the legs, and entertained them. "I like that one," you could imagine one girl saying to the other. "He is a joker, I think?"

He was a likeable man, perhaps 27 or 28, blue-eyed, fair-haired – all that kind of thing, but he had about him something that said, Keep Off. He was a little like a young hawk that hasn't got the hang of it, with a fluffy apprentice fierceness. And he was restless, always hooking and unhooking his legs, or flinging them hastily to one side to get them out of the way of someone coming past, or who seemed to sit too close. For a few days the three of them were together, usually in the early afternoon. When they left, a girl was on either side of him. But there ought to be a fourth, and soon there he was. When the four met, inside the café or on the pavement, it did not seem as if they had paired off. The girls still kept their eyes on the entertainer, their bright mouths smiling in anticipation for the moment they could laugh, for that's what they liked best to do. And he sat watching them laugh, pleased he was giving them what they wanted, and the other young man, who did not seem to hope for much, laughed too.

Once or twice they ate a proper meal. Sometimes they talked about a film they had seen. One afternoon he came in with a dark composed girl who had a sisterly and faintly satiric air. He bought her coffee and cakes and seemed apologetic about something. When the German girls came in he waved at them, tucked his legs in an awkward parcel to make room, and the three girls and the man stayed for a time, and then went off together. Thereafter I saw him with the dark girl and with other girls and he treated them as he did the German girls, for he seemed to like them all.

Once two tables outside were empty and I sat at one and soon he was at the other, dropping into a chair at the last moment as he went past, as if he might as well do that as anything else. By now we were café acquaintances. He remarked that the summer wasn't bad at all and he was glad he hadn't gone to Spain, for it was better here. There was a week left of his holiday. He worked at the builders' supply shop down the road. It wasn't bad, he quite liked it. Sitting close to him in the strong light I could see that he was older than he seemed. There were lines under his eyes, and he was often abstracted, as if he was continually being removed from present surroundings by an inner buzzer: attend to this.

The German girls arrived and they were laughing in anticipation before they sat down.

Then they were not coming to the café, and he was back at work. He dropped in once or twice with a colleague from work, two young men wearing very white boiler suits, which were to make them look knowledgeable about building materials. The German girls' young man seemed frail inside the thick suit.

One day I was standing outside the Underground station, waiting to meet someone. He strolled past, taking his time, preoccupied. Then his face spread in a smile so unlike anything I had seen there. I quickly turned. Just ahead of him was a small pale young girl with a pram. No, when you looked she was a small pale young woman, probably 20, and she was the baby's mother, from the tender way she bent to tuck it into already overwhelming covers. She smiled at the concealed baby, and then turned, startled, as the man came up and said in his whimsical, don't-take-me-seriously way, "Hilda, it's me." The two stood, dissolved in smiles. In a moment they would be in an embrace, but she recovered herself and quickly stood back. Then he, too, put on responsibility, as if fitting a winter's coat over his white boiler suit. Because he could not, apparently, embrace the mother, he leaned over the pram with a gallant air, and she leaned past him, lifted a bundle from its depths and held the baby so that he could see its face. He bent politely over it and made appropriate noises, laughing at himself so that she had to laugh too. But all the time his eyes were on the young mother.

She laughed again and pretended to thrust the baby at him for him to hold. At which he staggered back in a pantomime of an embarrassed male, and she fussed the bundle back under its covers and stood soberly, confronting him. He too was serious. They stood there a long time, long at least for an observer, perhaps a minute or more, looking at each other, entranced. These two were a match, a fit, the same kind: you had to say about them as you do, rarely, about a couple: they are two halves of a whole, they belong together.

Again it was she who recovered herself and pushed the pram away down the pavement. Slowly pushed. After a few steps she turned to look at him. On she went but turned again. He still stood there, gazing after her. She gave him a brave little wave, and went on. She went slower, slower ... but she had to go on, she had to, and she reached the corner much too soon, where she stopped and looked back to where he stood, his face as miserable as hers. Again the seconds sped past ... But at last she firmly pushed the pram on and away and disappeared. Never has there been a corner of a street as empty as that one. He stared. She had gone. He took two steps to go after her, then came back, sending over his shoulder a quick glance; yes, she really had gone.

Slowly he walked on, slower and stopped. He was level with me. He wasn't seeing anybody or anything, he was inside himself. He stood with his knees slightly bent, his arms loose, palms showing, his head back, as if he planned at some point to raise his eyes to the sky.

On the face of the charmed man chased emotions. There was regret, but a self-consciously dandyish regret, for even in his extremity he was not going to let go of this lifeline. There was bewilderment. There was loss. Above all, tenderness banishing the others. Meanwhile his forehead was tense and his eyes sombre. What was he thinking? "What was all that? What? But what happened...what *did* happen, I don't understand what happened...I don't understand..."

Something like that.

2 The story is both a narrative and a description. Which do you think is more important in the story?
What do you think is the main point of the story? Is it about a person, a place or an event, or all three?
Do you think the title of the story is a good one?
Do you think the story is the right length?
Does the length of the story reflect what the writer describes?

Write a brief summary of the storyline in about 50 words. Try to present only the facts without interpreting them.

3 The story has two distinct parts. Where is the turning point?
Much of the story involves a description of the two German girls. At what point did you realise that the story was about the young man?
How would you describe the mood of each part?

4 The story is written in the first person. Who is *I* likely to be: the writer, Doris Lessing, or a character that she has created?

At the beginning of the story, the writer describes the setting of the café as one which allows you to watch *soap operas*. These are serialised dramas on television or radio and are 'to be defined as a series of emotional events . . . to which you lack the key.' Do you think that, by the end of the story, the writer has found its key? Does she understand what has happened?

Do you think it's a good story? Did you enjoy it? Can you say why or why not?

5 Do you think the story could be presented in another form, such as a TV series, a play, a film or a poem? If so, choose one and decide which aspects of the story you would want to include, exclude or expand. You may like to try writing the script or the poem.